Strawberries
in November

Flowering Eastern Dogwood
(Cornus florida)

Strawberries in November

A Guide to Year-Round Gardening in the East Bay

BY JUDITH GOLDSMITH

with illustrations by the author

HEYDAY BOOKS, BERKELEY

Printed in the United States of America.

10   9   8   7   6   5   4   3   2   1

Published by Heyday Books
Box 9145
Berkeley, California 94709

ISBN: 0-930588-32-0

Cover Illustration: Janet Wood
Cover Design: Sarah Levin
Photograph on back page: Peggy Stokes
    T-shirt in photograph courtesy of
    Merritt College Landscape Horticulture Department
Interior design and production: Judith Goldsmith
Copyediting: Estelle Jelinek
Index: Judith Goldsmith

Illustrations on page vii are from the Historical Atlas of Alameda County by Thompson and West, originally published 1878.

CONTENTS

THANKS TO . . .

A guide that combines so many disciplines cannot be compiled without the help of a number of people. Special thanks go to Bob Raabe, professor of plant pathology at U.C. Berkeley; Tom Branca, horticulturalist and chair of Merritt College's Horticulture Department; and Barry Friesen, landscape contractor and former chair of Merritt College's Horticulture Department, for taking time out of their very busy schedules to review this manuscript and make suggestions; and also to Tom Branca for suggesting the need for an East Bay gardening calendar. Thanks must also go to the other caring and hard-working teachers at Merritt who gathered together and imparted to me a substantial part of the information presented in this guide: Jane Andrews, Judy Donaghey, Louis Biagi, Richard Orlando, and James Vlamis; and also, indirectly, to Emile Labadie, whose inspiration it was to found a department where gardeners could sharpen their horticultural skills.

Many thanks also to Jim Rosenau of Berkeley and Oakland's Revolutionary Garden Party for providing edible crops information, and to the many other Revolutionary Garden Party members and local gardeners who shared information on their successes and failures with different vegetables and fruit cultivars: Donna Mickleson, Tom Cumming, Rob Goodman, Lil Lee, Bill Savage, Ted Rosenkranz, Nancy Holland, Paula Krotser, Jeffrey Brown, Jacoba van Staveren, and Wayne Gallup. Also to Emil Lindquist, East Bay fruit tree propagator extraordinaire, who shared his fruit tree care knowledge; Dick Strahan, agricultural consultant, who contributed knowledge of East Bay agricultural history and crops; and Larry Stickney, of the San Francisco Mycological Society, who shared information on East Bay mushrooms. Thanks also to Don Forman of the Sierra Club for the idea of including mushrooms in the guide; to Sue Emmons for passing the idea for this guide on to me; to Stew Winchester of Diablo Valley College Landscape Horticulture Department for helping me locate photographs of seasonal blooms; to Bob Castro of Lakeside Park Gardens for information on banana fruiting and Bev Ortiz and Allan Kaplan of the East Bay Regional Park District for information on berry fruiting times; and to Malcolm Margolin of Heyday Books for getting as excited about this project as I am.

Finally, thanks to those who came before, who laid the groundwork on which my inspiration was built: Peter Berg and Peter Warshall; Helga and William Olkowski (*The City People's Book of Raising Food*), Lee Foster (*Backyard Farming*), and Jeanie Darlington (*Grow Your Own*); Pam Peirce and others at the San Francisco League of Urban Gardeners (SLUG); the Farallones Institute; Rosiland Creasy (*Edible Landscaping*) and Robert Kourik (*Designing and Maintaining Your Edible Landscape—Naturally*); the Berkeley Ecology Center (especially Gary Orkin's gardening column in the *Ecology Center Newsletter*); and Tilth (*The Future Is Abundant: A Guide to Sustainable Agriculture*). And, finally, thanks to the Oakland Library History Room.

Residence of W. B. Harrub, Fruit Vale, Alameda County, 1878

E. Lewelling's Residence and Fruit Farm of 120 Acres, San Lorenzo, Alameda County, 1878

PREFACE

It's December 22, the Winter Solstice, the day when sunlight is scarcest, yet the primrose in the sidewalk garden outside my window is adding still another yellow blossom to the hundred or so that have flowered since summer first began. There's been no frost even though this is midwinter, and there probably won't be more than a half-dozen short frosts for the entire year. A good part of the reason is the remarkable moderating effect of the California Current running close offshore. Because this broad ocean river maintains temperatures in the low fifties year-round, it rarely freezes here and seldom reaches the nineties in the summer. Considering that the San Francisco Bay Area is at almost the same latitude as Washington, D.C., on the opposite side of the continent, where snow falls every winter and summer days regularly exceed 100 degrees, the yearly temperature range here is a blessing. Gratitude to the primrose for reminding me.

It was during the industrial era that people changed from describing their home places in terms of being in a particular valley or mountain range and began to identify their homes in terms of political boundaries, such as "I'm from Detroit, Michigan, in the United States." Where once people had sensed a "spirit in the land" and believed the locales where they lived were alive, forests have now come to be regarded as board feet of lumber, mountains reduced to cubic yards of ore, and rivers diverted in gallons per minute. As a result, many of us only have a vague notion of the natural influences that surround us. It's not our fault; we weren't encouraged to believe that this information was useful. But if we are going to succeed in making the transition to an earth-centered epoch, we are going to have to begin rejoining our lives to lifeplaces.

Seeing the bioregional nature of the area we live in will help revive a more basic sense of our home places. Learning to know a place from this perspective helps us to learn the right way to live in it. And growing a garden is a good entry point for joining your particular home spot to your bioregion. Whether it's a full-scale household vegetable garden, a small plot of herbs, or even a bed of flowers, it will reveal from the beginning natural realities ranging from soil makeup and condition to the consequences of our unique (in North America) winter-wet/summer-dry climate.

I am glad to welcome the arrival of one of the first bioregional gardening guides to help our entry into this new epoch. May there soon be one for every unique bioregion!

Peter Berg
San Francisco
Alta California

Daffodils or Jonquils
(Narcissus)

*"Composting is collaborating with God
in converting the inevitable entropic drift
of the universe into . . . broccoli."*

The Revolutionary Garden Party

INTRODUCTION

Strawberries and nasturtiums in November? Carrots and potatoes in February? Lettuce and spinach and artichokes in July? The East Bay is an area of unique gardening possibilities. Here you can find tropical bougainvillea and purple princess flower from Brazil growing next to rhododendrons, dogwoods, and viburnums from colder climates. Palms and sagebrush native to Southern California and Mexico intermingle with pines, fir, and Port Orford cedar from Washington. Golden-flowered blackeyed Susan vine and delicate passion flower (from tropical Africa and tropical South America, respectively) climb contentedly, luxuriously up south-facing walls, while Boston ivy and Alpine Kenilworth ivy may be proliferating on the other side of the same house. Citrus, purple Mexican bush sage, and southern magnolias share our yards with English hawthorn, maples, Scotch moss and Scotch broom, and persimmon trees, and we don't even think twice about it. While gardeners in more severe climates watch their gardens thawing out in February or March and crocuses blooming through the snow, we have a year-round growing season and many annuals and bulbs that bloom right through the winter or return by themselves year after year.

For the gardener who knows its rhythms, and therefore how to take advantage of its possibilities, the East Bay can be an extravagantly bountiful place to garden. Salad and vegetable crops can be harvested right through the winter and summer, and gardens can be full of color all year round. Yet, to the newcomer or the inexperienced gardener, the East Bay can be confusing and frustrating. This guidebook has been written for you, to help you get attuned to this very special area and its unique rhythms and harmonies. You, the gardener (or would-be gardener), have to supply the energy and persistence, of course, and get out there and get your hands dirty, but with the knowledge of planting and pruning and watering and fertilizing times, your disasters can be minimized and your successes multiplied.

But you may wonder, why learn about natural cycles at all? Can't we live quite well without them?

The Cycles in Our Lives, or Why There Will Always Be Gardeners

Maybe as children we don't need to be aware of natural cycles. Summer can be wonderful and endless, school can be bothersome and endless, when it rains we stay indoors, and when it's clear and sunny we go to the beach or play outside. Even special holidays and birthdays and vacations have not yet fallen into a familiar pattern.

Maybe as urban dwellers we don't need to be aware of natural cycles. Food comes from the store, canned and processed; the weather forecast tells us whether to carry an umbrella or wear a jacket; we ride to work in a sheltered metal bubble; concerts and bookstores and movies go on year in and year out no matter the weather.

Maybe as modern people we don't need to be aware of natural cycles. Progress carries us ever forward, even sweeps us with it; what is a norm in our day was a vision in our grandparents'; work goes on forty hours a week, fifty or so weeks a year; we can mark time with raises, job changes, marriages, divorces, and children.

But as gardeners, we must be aware of our yearly and daily cycles, of the proper time and place for things. Finding bare-root asparagus to plant in midsummer is as impossible (even in our ultra-modern world) as trying to buy fresh sweet corn in January or cherries in October. Tomato plants planted in September will not survive to fruit; trying to gather dried flowers in December is hopeless; and so it goes in every contact with the earth's rhythms.

It's an unsolvable question whether we become aware of natural cycles because we like to garden or whether we like to garden because it makes us aware of natural cycles. Certainly food can now be purchased from huge agribusiness enterprises, flowers can be bought in flower shops, gardens can be planted with low-mainte-nance standard plants or even Astroturf or concrete, and we can even live in apartments or condominiums where lawns are watered on timers. No matter, some of us will always be gardeners. For the freshness of the food, for the joy of spring blooms, for the feel of earth, for the exercise, for the restoration of mistreated land, for the way it gets us back in touch with natural cycles; whatever the reason, some of us will always and forever want to plant and tend and nurture and harvest.

You undoubtedly know all this. You must have tried it yourself or thought about it, if you're looking through this book. And perhaps you've discovered, through trial and error, that to do it, and do it right, we need guides like this one, at least one for each local community. Plants are very sensitive to nuances of climate and surroundings; they won't bloom or fruit if things are not to their liking. But with a knowledge of their rhythms and needs, it's not hard to please them. Working with the seasons, you'll start your herbs early enough to get a good-sized plant by the end of summer, instead of buying or planting them near the end of their annual cycle; you won't try to plant cool-weather lovers when it's warm or warm-weather lovers just as it's turning cold. You'll know when to look for edible mushrooms, berries, or young greens. You'll buy your cantaloupes and artichokes when they're sweetest and be able to plan your meals around ripe in-season fruits and vegetables. In many, many ways, learning the rhythm of our green friends will help you to get more from them.

But, of course, there's more. Becoming aware of the rhythm makes us part of it, grounds us, and gives us a sustenance that doesn't come easily in this speedy, out-of-balance modern world. A link is reopened that has been closed, and the world becomes a more vital and exciting place. Watching for the first ladybug in spring, listening for the sound of sweet pea pods bursting like a corkscrew in the hot days of summer, testing an apple to see if it is ripe and nearly ready to fall, noting the first daffodils as they push their way up through the soil in winter—all of these make us feel closer to a vital force that is larger than the unpaid phone bill or the long lines at the supermarket. Then too there is the deep satisfaction of providing for ourselves, of raising foods we like, of gathering our very own flowers to put on the desk of someone we like to give pleasure to.

There are so many reasons for getting in touch with the earth's rhythms, and those are the real reasons for this book—not just the practicality of it, but also the contentment it brings. Along with the sound of rain on the roof while sitting in front of a crackling fire, or a bee buzzing from flower to flower, or fresh bread just out of the oven, we should never be living without these things. How could we ever have believed that we could?

Cities Covered by this Guide

(from north to south)

Richmond
San Pablo
El Cerrito
Kensington
Albany
Berkeley
Emeryville
Piedmont
Oakland
Alameda
San Leandro
Castro Valley (western)
San Lorenzo
Hayward (western)
Newark

Also useful for:
Pinole
Hercules
Rodeo
Crockett
Martinez
Pittsburg
San Francisco Peninsula
Coastal San Jose (around Mowry
    Slough, Mud Slough, Alviso
    Slough; Guadalupe River area
    between urbanized areas and the
    bay; around lower Stevens Creek
    and Adobe Creek)
Pacifica and Half Moon Bay
parts of Marin County
(El Sobrante, eastern Castro Valley,
eastern Hayward, parts of Union City,
and Fremont have climates similar to
that described in this calendar, but
average 15 to 25 degrees warmer in
the summer. Parts of Oakland and
Berkeley that lie in the upper hills get
somewhat warmer and colder.)

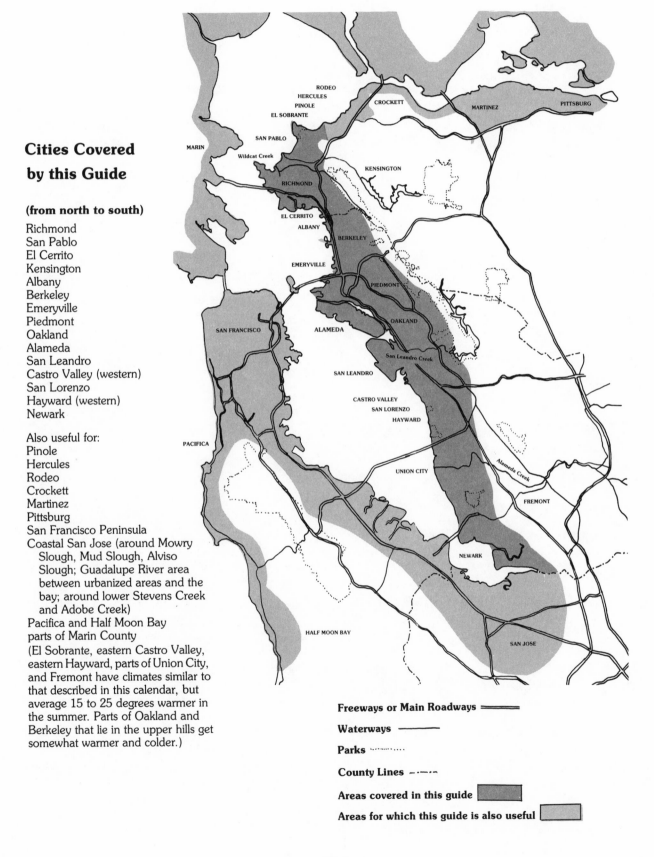

Freeways or Main Roadways ════

Waterways ────

Parks ···········

County Lines ─·──·──

Areas covered in this guide

Areas for which this guide is also useful

13

THE EAST BAY BIOREGION

Latitude 37° 52′ 24″ N   Longitude 122° 15′ 44″ W   Altitude 0-1,913 ft.

We live in a very special part of the universe, a unique "bioregion" known as the East Bay. The concept of a bioregion, developed by San Francisco eco-philosopher Peter Berg, refers to a geographic area having common characteristics of soil, watersheds, climate, and native plants and animals; that is, an area which has a unique interlocking web of life distinguishable from that of neighboring regions.

Gardening is a good way to connect with the ecology and rhythms of a particular place, and gardeners themselves can be an important force in helping an area to reach greater ecological health, when they learn which plants grow best and how to care for them so they thrive. "Make where you are a paradise" is one way to put it; if each of us works to plant properly and care for the soil and birds and insects *right in our own backyard,* the cumulative incremental change will eventually make this world, not to mention our own neighborhood, a nicer place. "Know thyself," the Delphic Oracle advised; we are finding today that this self-knowledge includes "know thy land" or "know thy bioregion." For gardeners it is especially important. So let us take an intensive look at the characteristics of this special area in which we find ourselves and in which we garden.

Climate

One of the qualities that makes the East Bay bioregion—which runs from Richmond in the north to Newark in the south—so unique is that we have mild and temperate weather very different from our neighbors. Contra Costa County to the east is much hotter in the summer and colder in the winter; Santa Clara County to the south is warmer and drier (only 13 inches of rain a year); and San Francisco, although

similar enough to use this calendar as a rule-of-thumb guide, is, in many sections, foggier and colder. We fall in *Sunset Western Garden Book*'s "Zone 17," along with Marin and Pacifica and Half Moon Bay, although Pacifica is much colder, and Point Reyes (in Marin) is much windier. All of these areas have in common the marine influence of an adjoining ocean, with winds coming predominantly from the ocean. But the Bay Area is a land of microclimates, where weather can be very different a few miles apart, and that makes each of these areas unique.

In the East Bay, our temperatures rarely go above 60 to 75 degrees or fall below 36 to 24 degrees. We have an extremely long growing season (average number of days between 32 degree temperatures): 333 days in Oakland, 306 in Hayward, 293 in Newark. Although we get seven to ten light frosts a year, our last prolonged freeze was in December 1972, when the temperature dropped to 23 degrees for an extended period, and many of the eucalyptus trees planted in the East Bay hills during the eucalyptus planting craze of 1904 died or developed frost

cracks; and we average only about four days a year with temperatures above 90. There is only 15 degrees of difference between the average temperature of our coldest month (January) and our warmest month (September); also only 15 degrees of difference between our average diurnal (within a 24-hour day) highest and lowest temperatures. (Orinda and Walnut Creek have a 25 to 26 degree range.)

It takes newcomers several years to notice our seasons, which are not the warm, hot, cool, and cold of other places in the U.S. Our biggest weather change is between a wet season and a dry. We share California's "Mediterranean" climate—warm, dry summers, and cool, wet winters—which is also typical of countries that surround the Mediterranean Sea, of western Australia, of coastal Chile, and of South Africa, all areas with a similar marine influence and all at about the same latitude from the equator. That is the reason why so many plants from these areas have been introduced here.

We get 18 to 20 inches of rain a year (compared with Southern California's 15 inches, the U.S. average of 30 inches, and the Santa Cruz Mountains' average of 60 inches), but nearly all of this rain falls from October to April. Of course there are occasional extremes: during the 1975-1977 drought, rainfall fell below 10 inches a year, while 1981–82, 1982–83, and 1985–86 were all extra-wet winters. January is our wettest month (with December and February close seconds), and July (along with August and September) our driest.

Our winds come predominantly from the direction of San Francisco Bay, and although not strong enough to make this a prime site for wind-farming, they can be quite strong right along the bay edge. There is a fairly strong afternoon wind in the summer, but in some spots we don't feel it because local topography or trees shield us.

Soil and Water

Another common characteristic of the East Bay watershed is our "Montmorillonite" clay soil, which shrinks in dry weather and swells in wet, causing house foundations to slip and crack. (Only the city of Alameda, the areas very near the eastern rim of the bay, and the floodplain areas along our creeks have sandier soil.) This clay soil is our biggest asset and greatest problem. If we didn't have clay soil to soak up and hold our sparse water, this area would be almost a desert. On the other hand, we have to add lots of organic material to our soil to get enough air space into it, not work it when it's wet, and wet it a little to be workable at all; and even with all this care, it can give our cultivated plants water mold root rots (though our natives have adapted and don't have this problem).

Most of our soil, as befits a dry climate, is only very mildly acid (typically about 6.5 pH in Berkeley and Oakland), so we don't need to add ash or lime as is common in the acidic soils of the much rainier eastern United States. (A heavy deposit of conifer needles from a tree above your property, however, can make your yard significantly more acid.) Most plants we want to grow are happy with such nearly neutral soils, so this low acidity is only a setback with the forest-native acid-soil-lovers like rhododendrons, azaleas, camellias, hydrangeas, fuchsias, primulas, pieris, and ericas, some of which have to be especially coddled, given extra large amounts of organic material, and checked for iron chlorosis (since they can absorb less iron from our more alkaline soils).

Our topsoil was reported as 3 to 4 feet deep in 1871 (fairly thin, actually, compared with the depth the first pioneers found when they settled the Midwest). Wells 14 to 35 feet deep were said to hit water back then. (Nowadays they might have to go down 100 to 150 feet.) But this water, and that running in our creeks, did not prove enough for the numbers who came to live here, so since the late 1920s our water has been brought in from the Camanche Reservoir on the Mokulumne River in the foothills of the

Sierra Nevada, by way of Briones and San Pablo Reservoirs. This water is said to be of extremely high quality, so that we rarely have to worry about salt buildup from irrigating our gardens or even our container plants.

Microclimates

Another distinguishing feature of the East Bay (which it does, however, share with other parts of the Bay Area) is that it is a land of microclimates, where growing conditions may be different from city to city, and from neighborhood to neighborhood, as well as the usual differences found on different sides of a house and in less sheltered or more sunny spots. From our highest point, Vollmer Peak in Tilden Regional Park (1,913 feet, from which all the creeks between Wildcat Creek in Richmond and San Leandro Creek in San Leandro flow), to the flatlands bordering San Francisco Bay, there are enough hills and valleys to make quite a few interesting climate variations. For example, there is Huckleberry Regional Preserve in the Oakland Hills, which gets warmer and cooler a few months earlier in the year than the area around it; Oakland's Eastmont/Oakknoll neighborhood, a warm valley where plums can be in full bloom in early January; North Oakland's "Banana Belt," a warm area around 52nd Street and Telegraph Avenue (the old "Temescal District," once the site of a very productive berry farm); "Palm Canyon," below Lake Temescal, another warm area where palms grow lavishly; and Wildcat Canyon, which gets frosts more often than its surroundings. Another example is West Berkeley, which is much cooler in summer than is North Oakland; thus West Berkeleyans can grow leafy vegetables easily in the summer, while gardeners in North Oakland have more success with hot weather lovers like tomatoes. If the plants you notice in your neighborhood consistently seem to start to bloom later or earlier than noted in this calendar, you may well be in a cooler or warmer microclimate zone (this guide should help you to figure this out, so you can plan your planting better). As they say in the Bay Area, "If you don't like the weather, walk [or move?] a few blocks."

Early History

Much of the land we now garden in the northern East Bay was once grassland (tall perennial native bunch grasses that stayed green in summer, unlike the exotic annuals that have now replaced them); only along the creeks did a variety of plants, including deciduous plants or others that needed water all year round, grow. Likewise, the southern part of the East Bay (from about San Leandro to Newark) was once almost all floodplain covered with willows and other riparian species; the water that once fed the area has been channelized or otherwise contained.

One of the big forces of transformation was the early farmers. From almost as soon as the Spanish and their cattle were "persuaded" to make way for the new settlers brought in by the gold rush, the East Bay was found to be a prime gardening area. In fact, Alameda County was such a good agricultural county that it was used as the model for turning California's Central Valley, and later Sonoma, Napa, and other counties, to agricultural production. Because of the mild climate and the high water table, it was found that a large variety of crops could be grown with "dry-farming" (nonirrigated) techniques, that is, using only natural rainfall for water. Certain types of fruit did very well here, and, in fact, areas that are now urbanized, such as the "Deaf and Blind School" campus in Berkeley (now part of U.C. Berkeley), the Fruitvale district of Oakland, and parts of Alameda and San Leandro, were covered with fruit trees in the 1880s.

In fact, four-fifths of Alameda County was once covered with farms that raised grain, produce, poultry, and livestock; and dried or canned crops were shipped from here all over the world. San Leandro is home of the caterpillar tractor, which was invented to break up that area's heavy soils. The "Hayward district" (the area from Oakland to Alameda Creek) produced more cherries than any other district in California; a popular though incorrect legend had it that the Bing cherry cultivar originated in the East Bay and was named for farmer William Meeks's Chinese cook, who first used them to make superb pies. Large crops of apricots were harvested, including a popular Alameda Helmskirk cultivar. Rhubarb grown around San Leandro was the main spring supply of that crop for the entire United States. North Oakland had the largest currant patches in the country and a currant- and berry-canning factory. Other agricultural tree crops included pears, plums, almonds, peaches, prunes, apples, chestnuts, olives, English walnuts, pecans, beechnuts, and hazelnuts; other fruit crops were strawberries, raspberries, loganberries, and blackberries; vegetables included peas, potatoes, tomatoes, onion, squash, cabbages, beets, cauliflower, celery, asparagus, table corn, pumpkins, sweet potatoes, and cucumbers.

East Bay Gardening: Advantages and Problems

In our beneficent climate, with its high minimum temperature and great variety of microclimates, many plants do well. The San Francisco Bay Area is in the overlap area between the Northern California–Oregon–Washington climate zone, and the Southern California–Baja California climate zone, and plants from both these areas can be grown here. It has been said, in fact, that more different kinds of plants grow successfully in the Bay Area than anywhere else in California (with the exception of the Santa Cruz Mountains), and we certainly can grow a good many of them in the East Bay.

The East Bay's mild climate is especially good for seed production, growing herbs, growing cut flowers for ornamental use (which used to be a flourishing business here not very many years ago), and growing many of the flowers and grasses used in dried arrangements. Food crops that do best are cool-weather lovers like artichokes, Brussels sprouts, fava beans, broccoli, cauliflower, cabbage, lettuce, etc. (see *September Vegetable Planting,* p. 64, for more suggestions).

A special feature of our climate is that, in most parts of the East Bay, we can grow these cool-weather crops right through the summer. In other ways too the East Bay can be said to have all-year-round horticultural possibilities. We can plant many plants through much of the year. Bulbs that have to be replanted anew each year after danger of frost is past

in more severe climates return on their own here. Also, some plants that grow as annuals in other locales (dying to the ground in winter and going to seed) or as deciduous plants (losing their leaves and going dormant each winter) become perennials and semi-evergreens here. Among the "annuals" and "deciduous" plants that thrive here nearly year-round are black-eyed Susan vine, nandina, euryops, Chinese elm, chasmanthe, pampas grass, rock cotoneaster, daylily, flowering tobacco, geraniums, sweet alyssum, English daisy, lobelia, nasturtium, and tomatillos.

But there are also a few disadvantages to our mild climate. In general, spring bloomers flower earlier here than in less temperate zones, but summer bloomers get started a bit later (and if we have a very foggy summer, may bloom very sparsely). And some plants, including apricots, peaches, apples, crocus, forsythia, lilac, pomegranate, melons, tomatoes, eggplants, peppers, okra, and Russian olive, need a bit of frost or more real heat and are not as happy here as in more extreme climates. Though cultivars of some of these are being developed that are more content with our weather, even cultivars of peach and apple especially bred for their low-chill requirements may still not get enough heat in our foggy summers to produce well. A good rule of thumb is that sour fruits do better here than sweet fruits, which need more heat (although your yard just might be a miniclimate that is an exception).

Gardeners also need to be aware that the East Bay has some unique plant pests and diseases. Powdery mildew, unlike other mildews which like wetter climates, finds our combination of warm days, cool nights, and low light levels (due to fog) just perfect and spreads rampantly. The best remedy is to plant susceptible plants in direct sunlight rather than in shaded areas. Plants which it loves to visit include flowering plants such as African violets, tuberous begonia, California poppy, calendula, columbine, crape myrtle, dahlias, euonymus, privet, roses, sweet pea, violas, pansies, and zinnias; trees such as crabapples, oaks, and sycamores; and food crops such as peas, peaches, beans, cucumber, squash, strawberries, apples, and grapes. Another very local pest is the cypress tip moth, rare elsewhere, which loves to invade our introduced species of cypress (*Chamaecyparis* genus), juniper (*Juniperus* genus, including the Hollywood juniper and all ground cover junipers), and arborvitae (*Platycladus* genus). Juniper twig girdler, which causes tip yellowing and dieback on Hinoki cypress and on junipers, is also not found anywhere else. We also get more than our share of peach leaf curl and brown rot of stone fruits, walnut blight, and phytophthora water mold root rots, though these are not special to just the East Bay. Aren't we lucky? But actually we have much fewer plant diseases than wetter places.

The Rhythms and Harmonies of an East Bay Year

Despite these few problems, we gardeners of the East Bay have had great success. We've transformed the look of this area greatly and will probably continue to do so as long as there are seeds to sow. We can do even better if we keep in touch with our bioregion's special rhythms and harmonies. So let's take a "walk through the seasons" in the East Bay.

The East Bay's growing year really begins in September and October, the traditional time the early farmers in this area would plant their crops for growth using just natural rainfall for irrigation. As the nights get cooler but the ground is still warm, this is the optimum time to start seedlings of leafy vegetables and root crops and to plant almost anything (except warm-season crops). If you keep planting more seedlings or starting seeds throughout September, October, and November, you'll stagger your harvesting times in the spring months ahead.

We have only a very brief autumn in the East Bay, between early November and Thanksgiving, and very few plants that get good fall color in our mild climate. Nourished by the rains of October to April, however, bulbs, annuals, and grasses perk up their heads, making February through May a riot of flower color in both the wilds and our gardens.

As the weather warms in March, we can start getting flowering and fruiting vegetable seedlings going, to be set out in April. If we plant leafy vegetables now, they may grow well, or we may get a period of unusually warm weather that will cause them to bolt and go to seed. With the right cultivar, however (see Resource Guide, p. x, for suggestions), chances of success are much higher than in warmer summer areas. (Or hedge your bets and plant both, getting good warm-season crops if we get an unusually warm spell, or good cool-season crops if the weather stays cool.) Looking at the other side of the picture, warm-season crops are best set out through April and May, so they can get big and bushy and put out plenty of fruit, ready to start to ripen in late July to early August; but trying to get tomato or eggplant or pepper seeds or even seedlings going in July or later will mean that just as they start really fruiting, the rains may beat them down.

June and July starts our dry season, and now the difference between our wild areas and our gardens begins to show. In the hills, flowers and grasses are drying and turning brown, whereas in our gardens, aided by our watering, exotic plants keep on blooming and subtropicals not even adapted to this area come into full and glorious bloom. But it's not until September and October, our "second spring," that they get the full heat they love and really put on a show, and that corn, peppers, tomatoes, eggplants, and other warm-weather-lovers can ripen fully.

And then it's the rainy season again . . .

(For a more detailed, and very descriptive, explanation of San Francisco Bay Area weather, I highly recommend *Weather of the San Francisco Bay Area* by Harold Gilliam [Berkeley: University of California Press, 1962].)

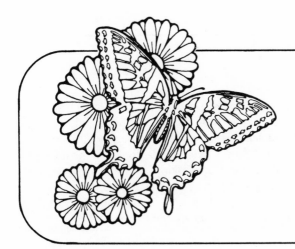

HOW TO USE THIS CALENDAR GUIDE

This guide to the East Bay may be used for at least three purposes: learning about the plants you see around you, planning your own garden, and caring for and maintaining your garden.

Learning About the East Bay's Plants

Walking around in the East Bay can be an exciting adventure if you get to know the plants that live here. Instead of a mass of undifferentiated green, you'll be greeting old friends, noticing which are in bloom or going to fruit, which are or are not doing well. If you notice a plant in bloom everywhere during a particular month, you can use the Bloom Lists included in this guide to help you identify what it is. First, try to decide if the plant is a tree, shrub, ground cover, herbaceous perennial, annual, or bulb.

Tree: Usually a single-trunked woody perennial that grows over 15 feet in height.

Shrub: A multitrunked woody perennial that grows to 15 or 20 feet or less, but grows taller than a ground cover.

Ground Cover: A woody or nonwoody perennial, usually no more than 3 feet in height, which naturally spreads out horizontally, making a good covering for bare ground.

Herbaceous Perennial: A nonwoody plant which lives for more than one year, usually fairly low-growing, often grown for its flowers.

Bulb: A herbaceous, usually flowering, plant which grows from a bulb or corm or other large root; in our climate, many bulbs are perennial.

Annual: A herbaceous plant which must be reseeded anew each year; there are relatively few cultivated plants which are annuals in our climate.

Weed: A weed is a plant in the wrong place, say weed lovers who feel weeds haven't gotten the respect they deserve for renewing our soil; but in this guide's Bloom Lists this category includes introduced low-growing plants, annual or perennial, which grow without human care or attention.

If you don't find the plant you're looking for under the Bloom List subhead where you think it should be, move around a little; maybe the plant grows taller than the one you saw, or maybe it becomes woody as it grows older and therefore is under shrubs or ground covers instead of under herbaceous perennials. You also need to check the category "Natives," which includes plants in all the above categories; however, natives are usually found nowadays in the hills and along creeks, rarely in the cultivated gardens of our urbanized areas.

Besides looking at other categories of plant types to find your plant, you should look backward and forward a month or two; the Bloom Lists indicate only the start of each plant's bloom time. Also check the All-Year Bloomers List at the end of this section, since it might just be a plant that blooms intermittently throughout the year in the East Bay.

The Bloom Lists are arranged in alphabetical order by botanical name, so that they will be useful to professionals who are looking for a specific plant. They list first the common name of each plant, and then the Latin/scientific/botanical name. Often the common name is quite imprecise, such as that of black-eyed Susan and black-eyed Susan vine, plants which have no similarity other than yellow-orange flowers with black centers. The botanical name is what you really need to know if you want to find out more information on a plant; that is how the plant will be listed in most plant books. If no common name is listed, that means there isn't one, and usually the genus name is used as the common name, such as *Camellia reticulata* and *C. japonica* (when the same genus name is used one right after the other, it is commonly abbreviated), which are both commonly called "Camellia." If many species of the same genus have the same common name, the botanical listing says "*Ceanothus* sp." to include all of them. After the genus and species names, you may sometimes find the name of the variety (always lower case) or the cultivar (always capitalized and between single quotes). A *variety* is a naturally occurring, usually geographically localized, variant of a plant, which can be propagated by seed. A *cultivar* (abbreviated cv.) is a variety of plant which has been isolated and developed by humans; it is propagated by cuttings and usually does not reproduce exactly by seed.

There is only room in the Bloom Lists to indicate bloom color and occasionally shape, size, or noticeable fragrance. So, you'll need to use them in conjunction with Sunset's *Western Garden Book,* or any one of the many plant guidebooks with good pictures for a fuller description of the plant. Such guidebooks can also tell you whether the plant tolerates shade or drought, how big it gets, and where it comes from; they will not, however, tell you when the plant blooms or fruits in the East Bay, which is what this guide does.

Finally, another problem inherent in this guide is the fact that any given year may have early- or late-arriving seasons. In a year with early warm weather, such as 1986 was, you'll have to adjust the information given here by looking a month or even two months ahead to find out what's blooming. For the most success, try to stick to identifying plants as they start to come into full bloom.

Planning Your Garden

The Bloom Lists can help you find plants to put in your garden for color at various times of the year. If your garden looks dull and dead in late summer (like many in the East Bay), a look at the list will introduce you to *Zauschneria* or naked lady or plumbago. Only plants that are generally known to grow well in the East Bay are included in the Bloom Lists, so they can also help give you ideas for other plants to consider planting.

The Bloom Lists can also aid in discovering when a particular plant should be obtained. It's a good idea to put plants into the ground not too long before their period of active growth, so that they will put out roots and shoots and not perplex you as to whether they are dying or just going into dormancy. Bulbs, in particular, can be obtained only within the several-month period before they bloom. To find bulbs to plant in late fall for spring or summer color, look through the Bloom Lists under bulbs for February through August; bulbs for fall planting can be found in the November through February Bloom Lists. (If you're mail-ordering bulbs, nurseries will have included only plants for the next season in their spring or fall catalog; similarly, nurseries will usually carry plants when they can be planted. However, if there's a particular plant you'd like to plant, finding out when it blooms can be a help in figuring out when to check for it in nurseries and mail-order catalogs.)

The Bloom Lists can also help clear up confusion about which plants are annuals and which are perennial in the East Bay. So many plants listed in seed catalogs and gardening books as annuals actually grow as perennials here that it can get quite confusing. The plants may disappear or go dormant, but their roots stay alive and they return the following year. A few, like nasturtiums, reseed themselves so well that we don't have to replant them for that reason. Only plants which must indeed be replanted anew each year in the East Bay are listed as "annuals" in this guide. If a plant is not listed here as an annual, you can hope for it to come back year after year, wherever it was planted in your yard, unless of course it encounters disease or environmental problems.

Finally, the Bloom Lists will also tell you when to shop for particular plants in order to see them during their time in bloom; this is important for picking from the many cultivar color variations now available.

Caring for Your Garden

If you want to use this guide to plan garden jobs, it's a good idea to read through all the monthly descriptions first. Maybe you'd like to prune some of the trees in your backyard: You'll discover that it's best to wait until November to January to prune fruit trees and other deciduous plants and that Japanese maple should never be pruned in the spring. A general read-through could also point out that it would be better to put off buying that wisteria you want until it's available bare-root.

After acquainting yourself with these general guidelines, reread the monthly descriptions in the month they refer to in order to find out what needs to be done or can best be done that month. When doing this, also check back to the previous month and forward to the next month to see if there is something you forgot or something coming up that you want to get ready for. As you use this guide, you'll start to get a feeling for the East Bay's rhythm and be able to use the monthly descriptions as just a quick reminder. Write in the margins if you like, and keep track of how things worked best in your garden.

Where to Find "How To" Information

This guide does not include comprehensive "how to" information. In order to do that, it would have to be much larger; besides, there are already many sources for that information. Some suggestions:
- *Sunset Western Garden Book*
- *Sunset Introduction to Basic Gardening*
- many other Sunset books
- many HPBooks
- *Edible Landscaping* by Rosalind Creasy
- *Designing and Maintaining Your Edible Landscape— Naturally* by Robert Kourik
- Rodale's *Organic Gardening Magazine*

Instead, this guide gives the "when to" information for a very specific geographic area, something which no other source does for the East Bay. Used in combination with information gained from the above sources, which are so general that they cannot pin down specific times for garden jobs or bloom times for any one of the many geographic areas they cover, this guide can be a powerful resource.

A Note About Gardening Styles

This guide is written for both "traditional" gardeners and a new breed of gardener who has lately been emerging. The traditional gardener, possibly more accustomed to the planting patterns of other parts of the U.S., tends to plant dahlias, marigolds, primula, chrysanthemums, and other bulbs and annuals twice a year for color; and such perennials as hydrangeas, gardenias, azaleas, and fuchsias, plants which, in California's dry summer months, need quite a bit of hand-watering to bloom well. If that's your pattern, this guide includes information on the planting and care of these traditional favorites.

However, in recent years, especially since the 1975-77 drought, more and more gardens are being planted with a backbone of California natives and perennials, which do not need to be laboriously re-planted and hand-watered each year. Planting time for native wildflowers (September and October especially) are noted; perennials can be planted almost any time, though the best times are also mentioned. So, if your gardening interest falls more in the second category, read through the Bloom Lists for ideas for perennials and natives (with a good picture book to help you), and don't be put off by the descriptions of annual and bulb planting that are sprinkled through these pages. Gardening need only be as much work as you decide to make it!

enters the first and fifteenth degree of each zodiacal sign. Four of these, which fall midway between the Solstices and the Equinoxes, are shown on modern calendars as "the start of" each season, and they are noted in this guide to help give an idea of how the East Bay's seasonal pattern fits into the solar seasonal pattern.

Developing Your Own Internal Guide

A calendar guide such as this one has, to my knowledge, not been written before for the East Bay, and for good reason. Our weather varies enough from year to year that you can easily get several different opinions on bloom times for various plants, and optimum times for garden jobs. No guarantee can be given that the information collected here is perfect for any given year. However, it is much better than having no guide and can be the ground work for developing a system of your own. Take it as a good rule of thumb, as the kind of good advice you might get if you had the time to talk to several dozen ardent local gardeners. Then, season it with what you learn in your own garden, pass on what you know to other would-be gardeners, and . . . keep planting!

We'd like to hear from you about your experiences with gardening in the East Bay. What worked and what didn't? What special tricks have you discovered? What local sources have you found especially useful? Since microclimates have such a strong effect on local gardening, please be sure to include either your address or a nearby street intersection when you write, so that we can establish what type of microclimate your experiences apply to. Write to East Bay Gardening Guide, Heyday Books, Box 9145, Berkeley, CA 94709.

The Turning Points of the Year

A number of "turning points" in the solar year are noted in this guide with which you may not be familiar. Most of us know about the Solstices (June 21 and December 22), the days of the year that have the most and least daylight hours and when the sun rises furthest to the north and furthest to the south and sets furthest in the opposite direction. These are also commonly called Midsummer's Day and Midwinter's Day. You may also be familiar with the Equinoxes (March 20 and September 23), the days when daylight and darkness are equal and the sun rises due east and sets due west. But there is another set of turning points as well: the days on which the sun

All-Year Bloomers

These plants bloom sporadically throughout much of the year in the East Bay, so they cannot be listed under a particular season.

Blue Hibiscus (*Alyogyne huegelii*): shrub with purple-lavendar flowers

English Daisy (*Bellis perennis*): weed/herbaceous perennial

Red Valerian (*Centranthus ruber*): weed/herbaceous perennial

Mock Strawberry (*Duchesnea indica*): ground cover with yellow flowers

Fleabane (*Erigeron karvinskianus*): ground cover

Transvaal Daisy (*Gerbera jamesonii*): herbaceous perennial

Trailing Lantana (*Lantana montevidensis*): ground cover

Lion's Tail (*Leonotis leonurus*): perennial with orange tubular flowers in whorls

Sweet Alyssum (*Lobularia maritima*): herbaceous perennial

Geranium (*Pelargonium* sp.): herbaceous perennial/ground cover

Rose-carpet Knotweed (*Polygonum capitatum*): ground cover

Bird-of-Paradise (*Strelitzia reginae*): herbaceous perennial

Princess Flower/Pleroma (*Tibouchina urvilleana*): shrub

Nasturtiums (*Tropaeolum majus*): annual

A Note of Caution

Many plants are suggested as having edible parts in this book, including mushrooms, common weeds, and plants grown as ornamentals. If you have never tasted these before, be sure to use extreme caution; many people have moderate to severe reactions to even common food plants. So please be sure you have identified the plant absolutely correctly by using other guidebooks that have detailed descriptions; and if you're trying something for the first time, try only a little bit, and save a sample of the plant in case you have a reaction and have to explain to a doctor what the plant was.

JANUARY

Rain, rain, and more rain . . . in between the days of warm, sunny spring weather, the year's beginning is still mostly a time for staying indoors. January should be a quiet time, suitable for recovering from the holidays; but already the hills are starting to turn green, as well as our own backyards.

The winter is over, almost before it's begun. Leaves are still falling off trees, while new spring blossoms poke through the ground. About the second week, the **flowering quince,** the first new year's bloomer, can be seen here and there around the East Bay, bursting with salmon-colored flowers on otherwise bare branches. The first **crocus** also raises its cheerful head, and the **narcissus/daffodil** comes into bloom. Before another week goes by, these are joined by bright yellow flowers of that East Coast favorite, the **forsythia,** though that plant is not commonly planted here, since in our climate the leaves come out almost at the same time as the flowers and the bloom is not as dramatic as in areas with colder weather. But the really noticeable sign of spring in the East Bay has become the blooming of those now-numerous imports from Australia's Mediterranean climate zone, the **acacia** trees, which suddenly explode with bright yellow at this time.

The close of the dormant season, the first signs of spring—January is a transition month. In the East Bay it is also the time when cats start prowling, knocking container plants off porches. It's time to check pantry flour and grain jars for grain moths, which hatch around now. But winter is not over yet; this month has the greatest number of frosts.

FERTILIZING

Deciduous fruit trees need fertilizing two to three weeks before they bloom, and that means late January or very early February in the East Bay.

PLANTING

This is a prime month to buy **bare-root** trees, deciduous plants including roses and many fruit trees (see *December Planting,* p. 79, for list), which have been dug up during their dormancy and shipped to the nurseries. Buying these shrubs and trees bare-root is much cheaper than buying them when they are repotted for sale in late February, and you'll probably be getting healthier plants too.

If the weather is dry, January is a good time to dig up and move plants that are in the wrong place (i.e., too shaded or too sunny); however, any dry period into February is good for this.

Just after the new year is a good time to get out seed catalogs and order cool-season vegetable seeds for your spring and summer garden. If you want to grow **Japanese anemones** for fall color, now is a good time to start them, as they need a long growing period before they bloom.

Violas, Pansies, and Johnny-Jump-Ups

(Viola sp.)

PRUNING

Your all-too-short holiday break is the prime and perfect time to prune **roses** and other deciduous plants (any clear day in January will do). Roses are cut back now in order to encourage new growth and big blooms and discourage ranginess, but especially to remove any infected parts that will reestablish diseases (such as rust and powdery mildew) during the next growing season. Be sure to clear the area thoroughly of all the prunings after your work is completed. If you're not sure how to prune roses properly, the East Bay Rose Society (current phone number available from Lakeside Park Garden Center, 832–9329), the Oakland Parks and Recreation Department (273–3866), and Merritt College Horticulture Department (436–2418) usually give demonstrations.

Other deciduous plants that need pruning now include fruit trees. **Peach, nectarine,** and **plum** in particular need heavy pruning all over every year to keep their growth within bounds. How to go about pruning them is less critical than with other fruit trees, as they sprout prolifically and won't be badly damaged no matter what you do. **Cherries** and **pears** need less pruning, but more care not to harm the buds. **Apples** need the least pruning but great care not to harm the buds; watersprouts and suckers need to be removed and horizontal growth that is likely to produce fruit encouraged. To prune cherries, pears, or apple trees for maximum fruit production and for properly shaping the trees' growth, you really need to know what you're doing. Again, Merritt College Horticulture Department usually gives demonstrations; if you can't attend a class, your local nursery probably stocks an inexpensive book, which can at least give you the basics of fruit tree pruning. Or call Merritt College Horticulture Department to hire a trained gardener.

Grapes, wisteria, passion vines, and other deciduous vines should also be pruned at this time (during dormancy) to discourage overgrowth and to keep them thinned so that sunlight can get in; in addition, this prevents layers of dead material accumulating and overburdening their support. January is also a good time to prune **fig** trees without disturbing either their early summer or late summer crop, though they rarely need to be pruned. However, do not prune ornamental deciduous plants yet (such as **flowering plum, flowering quince, crabapples, crape myrtle, jacaranda, hybrid roses, pyracantha, *Buddleia, Albizia,* trumpetvine, *Deutzia,* forsy-** thia, *Spiraea,* and *Weigela*). Wait until during or after they bloom since they put their flowers out on "old" wood (wood grown during the last growing season) and need a year's growth to bloom well.

OTHER CARE

Kitchen-window bulbs like shallots and chives, which went into dormancy last summer, may perk up now and start to grow. **Deciduous fruit trees** may need a follow-up dormant spray by early February (see *November Diseases* for description). Signs of the fuchsia gall mite (distortion of leaves and roots) may be appearing on your **fuchsias** now. This Brazilian insect (which first appeared in the Bay Area in 1981 and is now making fuchsia-growing extremely difficult) is active during low temperatures. You can attempt to control it by cutting off and destroying diseased parts; but insecticides are the only well-known control so far.

HARVESTING

The harvest may seem thin right now, but actually root crops including **parsnips, salsify, celery root (celeriac), potatoes, turnips, rutabaga, beets, Jerusalem artichokes,** and possibly even **carrots,** as well as leafy crops such as **collards** (which are sweetest in cold weather), **kale, leek, lettuce, cabbage, Swiss chard, broccoli,** and **cauliflower** should be available from a fall-planted garden. Supplement them with **sprouts** grown indoors. Sprouts from beans such as azuki, fava, garbanzo, lima, mung, pinto, and soy; other legume seeds such as alfalfa, clover, fenugreek, and lentils; leafy vegetable seeds including beets, Brussels sprouts, cabbage, cauliflower, celery, cress, kale, lettuce, parsley, purslane, and radish; grains seeds of barley, corn, millet, oats, brown unpolished rice, rye, wheat, and buckwheat; and other seeds including caraway, dill, flax, onion, pumpkin, peanut, safflower, and sunflower all make tasty winter salad additions. Don't eat large quantities of sprouts from beans or legumes, however.

Dancy tangerines are in season January to April in Northern California, and the stores should also have many other tangerines. By mid-January, **fennel** should also be available at the markets. **Artichokes,** though available all year, are at their best in the cold season, when slow growth allows their full flavors to develop. Frost-burned ones are considered to be even better.

RECIPES

Brazilian Feijoada
with Spinach-Kale Salad

Serves 8

Feijoada is traditionally a meal with many different dishes; this is a simplified but very tasty version.

Black Beans with Rice

1 lb dried black beans
¼ lb salt pork or sausage (optional)
1 onion, sautéed
garlic
3 tomatoes, chopped (optional)
1–2 hot peppers, chopped (optional)
cilantro (optional)
salt and pepper to taste

Soak beans overnight in 2 quarts of water.

Next day, bring beans to boil and simmer 2 hours or more, with the other ingredients.

Serve over ordinary rice, or make **Brazilian Rice:** boil enough rice for eight, then add to it a sautéed mixture of onion, garlic, tomatoes, paprika, and roasted peanuts.

Serve with orange sections, lime to squeeze over the Black Beans, and Spinach-Kale Salad.

Spinach-Kale Salad

½ small bunch kale
½ small bunch spinach
Dressing:
2 tsp Dijon-style mustard
½ tsp sugar
¼ tsp pepper
½ tsp salt
6 Tb olive oil
3 Tb red wine vinegar
Garnish:
½ cup crushed peanuts (may be toasted)
1 cup sliced hearts of palm

Cut or tear kale and spinach into bite-size pieces; prepare dressing by combining all ingredients, dress salad, and serve with garnish.

Chinese Mustard Greens Soup

Serves 4 to 6

1 bunch mustard greens
4 large Shitaki mushrooms (or 4 large button mushrooms)
1 can (about 14 oz) chicken broth
¾ tsp sugar
2 tsp soy sauce
2 to 4 thin slices ginger root
2 cups water
2 Tb finely sliced green onions

If you're using dried Shitaki mushrooms, soak them in warm water to cover until softened.
Tear or cut greens to bite-size pieces.
Heat all other ingredients (except green onions), with 2 cups water in saucepan.
When mushrooms are soft (20-30 minutes), cut to bite-size, and add to saucepan with liquid they were soaking in.
Simmer 25 minutes or as long as possible.
Add greens and simmer 3 more minutes.
Add green onions and simmer 2 more minutes.

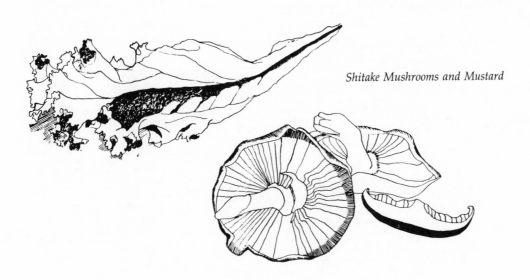

Shitake Mushrooms and Mustard

PLANTS WHICH START TO BLOOM IN JANUARY

Trees
Bailey's Acacia (*Acacia baileyana*):yellow

Shrubs
Darwin Barberry (*Berberis darwinii*): golden yellow
Sasanqua Camellia (*Camellia sasanqua*): white, pinks, reds
Camellia reticulata: white, pinks, reds
Cameliia japonica (some cultivars): white, pinks, reds
Woolly Senna (*Cassia tomentosa*): yellow
Japanese Flowering Quince (*Chaenomeles japonica*): salmon to red on bare branches
Winter Daphne (*Daphne odora*) pink and fragrant
Poinsettia (*Euphorbia pulcherrima*): red (its natural bloom time)
Menzies' Hebe (*Hebe menziesii*): white lilac
Saucer Magnolia (*Magnolia soulangiana*): huge white flowers on bare branches
Evergreen Pear (*Pyrus kawakamii*): white
African Linden (*Sparmannia africana*): white + yellow, then orange, then red stamens

Ground Covers
Cape Weed (*Arctotheca calendula*): yellow daisylike
Mediterranean Heather (*Erica carnea*): rose (+ white, red, pink cvs.)
Bergenia-white, rose, lilac, or purplish (+ cvs.) clusters among big leaves

Vines
Primrose Jasmine (*Jasminum mesnyi*): yellow

Herbaceous Perennials
Rock Cress (*Arabis* sp.): white, pink, rose-purple
Cineraria (*Senecio stellata*): blues, purples (+ white, pink cvs.)

Annuals
Nasturtium (*Tropaeolum majus*): orange
Fairy Primrose (*Primula malacoides*): white, pink, lilac, purple, or white against ferny leaves
Poor Man's Orchid (*Schizanthus pinnatus*): rose, pink, lilac, purple, or white against ferny leaves

Bulbs
Daffodils and Jonquils (*Narcissus* sp.): white

Bailey's Acacia
(Acacia baileyana)

FEBRUARY

By February 1, Northern California usually has had 60 percent of its annual rainfall, although occasionally this can be the rainiest month. There may also be a dry or warm spell such as we had in 1985, but don't be fooled; some rain is still ahead. Because of this, an early warm spell now can do harm by breaking plant dormancy and thus wreak havoc with flower and fruit development and diseases. In fact, a cold February is supposed to indicate a fruitful year. So finish the last winter chores, try to take advantage of the first spring opportunities, and enjoy the early bloomers as they each put on their show.

Deciduous **magnolias**, which started to stir during January, can be seen opening their huge cup-and-saucer blooms on bare branches. Toward the end of February or early March, they'll be in full bloom. Visit them at the west entrance to the U.C. Berkeley Botanical Garden (where you can also catch African Hill at the height of its color) or at Strybing Arboretum's entrance in San Francisco. Another spectacular early February show is the blooming of the **almond trees**, then the **apricot trees**, and then the pink and the white **flowering plums**, as spring officially commences on February 5. The **pear** also begins to put out its rose, then white blooms, at the same time as its leaves unfold; not too long after, fruiting **peaches** and **nectarines** begin to show their white, pink, or red buds. Right around February 15, **avocado** trees join them. Lawns that appear uninteresting most of the year are covered with the bright yellow wildflowers of **Bermuda buttercup**. California natives which come into bloom at this time are **ceanothus 'Julia Phelps,' leatherwood, fuchsia-flowered gooseberry**, and **pink-flowering currant**. The native **buckeye** also greets the season by sprouting its first green leaves; **willows**, **elderberries**, and other deciduous plants also begin to leaf out. As the weather warms, birds also start to return, and you can hear them for the first time in the morning. In the East Bay,

it's time to get that spring garden going!

PRUNING

"After Washington's birthday" (February 22) is the time to prune **fuchsias**, before they start to bloom on "new wood" (branches grown this year).

Houseplants are also beginning their spring growth. February is a prime time to repot indoor plants that have gotten too big for last year's container, scarify (roughen the exterior surface of) the root ball if the plant has become rootbound (roots trying to escape out the drainage hole and/or circling around the inner edge of the pot), prune, fertilize, and hose off.

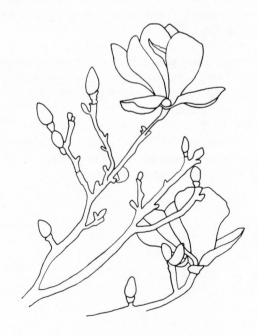

Saucer Magnolia
(Magnolia soulangiana)

PLANTING

Now is the time to buy, but not yet to plant, "summer-flowering" **bulbs** (see *May to August Bloom Lists*). These will not be available after early March.

Early February is also your last chance to buy deciduous trees and shrubs **bare-root**; by mid-February they will be potted up and priced higher. Plant them as soon as possible.

In February, you can start seeds of **cool-season vegetables** (see *March Planting*, p. 36) in flats indoors or in a cold frame for an early spring crop. Also, if you have **seeds** left from past years, this is a good time to test them by sprinkling a few between damp paper towels and discarding those batches that don't start to sprout in a reasonable period. (Check vegetable-growing books to find out the seed-sprouting period for each plant.) In general, seeds from onion and members of its family need to be ordered fresh each year. Seeds from lettuce, parsley, salsify, sweet corn, and parsnips should be planted within two years. If kept dry, these seeds should last 3 to 5 years: asparagus, beans, cabbages, carrots, celery, chicory, endive, okra, peas, peppers, radishes, and spinach. Seeds good for 5 or more years (if kept dry and at room temperature) include beets, cucumbers, mustard, and tomatoes. (Note that not all the seeds mentioned above should be planted now, but you may want to test their viability now to decide if you ought to order them or not.)

During February you may also want to order seeds for **warm-season vegetable** crops (see list under *March Planting*); however, if you're not planning an early start this year, you can wait until March or even April to order them.

If there is a dry spell and if your soil was not already prepared last fall, dig in hot fertilizers (chicken or rabbit manure, bloodmeal) to let them break down a bit before April planting of warm-season crops.

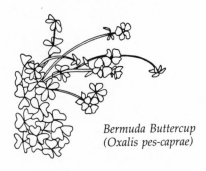

*Bermuda Buttercup
(Oxalis pes-caprae)*

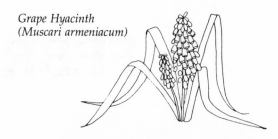

*Grape Hyacinth
(Muscari armeniacum)*

INSECTS AND OTHER UNWELCOME GUESTS

February is *the* month to catch **snails** before they breed and multiply. Snails become active and come out at night only when nighttime temperatures stay above 40 to 45 degrees F; check an outdoor thermometer to see when the time has arrived. An old East Bay resident told me how it was done in the early days: An old tarp or cloth was spread on the ground with a low dish containing meat juice on it. There's probably not much else for those hungry snails just coming out of dormancy to eat yet, because they all head right for the meat juice. Then you go out about 10 or 11 p.m. with a flashlight, and either toss them into a bucket or otherwise dispose of them.

Another method is the citrus trap. Half-grapefruit rinds are set around the garden, lifted on one side by a stick. Snails gather inside, where you can find them. Other attractants are fresh granulated yeast or beer, which also contains yeast.

Snail hunting is unpleasant on still-cold February evenings, but diligence in this task now, and through March if necessary, may save you many times as much work later in the year (although some gardeners find that snails migrate from other yards, so the vigilance has to continue). Cleanup and weeding as the weather warms in March and the weeds start to grow also help keep the numbers down. U.C. Agriculture Co-op Extension (881-6341 or 644-4345) has a booklet on how to prepare our garden snails for gourmet eating, if you want to try that route.

HARVESTING

February is the leanest month of all, but on a clear day you may be inspired to get out and collect some wild new spring shoots for **salad greens** (and do some weeding at the same time?). In the old days, this was the peak time for dairy products, as cows grazed on fresh green grass, and their milk and butter were especially high in vitamin A. Nowadays, dairy products are pasteurized, which destroys the vitamin content, and the vitamins are replaced in constant quantities all year. Another big harvest in the past at this time of year used to be San Francisco Bay crabs (the season opens in December), but the catch is nothing like it used to be. You could commemorate these past bounties by making traditional New England chowder or seafood bisque. But as a gardener, you might want to try a Dutch favorite, Kruudmoes, which showcases the young greens just coming up; or cook some of your new young endive shoots into a delicious cream- and cheese-sauce Chicken au Gratin.

Heuchera

or Alum Root

RECIPES

Kruudmoes

Serves 4

A very old peasant recipe from the eastern part of Holland, this dish is traditionally eaten in early spring when the first green shoots of vegetables and herbs appear in the garden.

1 cup barley
½ to ¾ lb sausage, traditionally guelder or frankfurter, but knockwurst is great (optional)
¼ cup finely chopped green herbs (chervil, chives, celery, sorrel, or others you might be growing)
1 cup raisins
1 pint buttermilk
maple syrup or molasses

Simmer barley in 1 quart water for 1½ hours (uncovered).

For the last ½ hour, add sliced sausage.

For the last ¼ hour, add herbs and raisins.

When all or most of the water is absorbed or evaporated, remove from heat and stir in buttermilk.

Traditionally eaten cold or lukewarm (though also good warm) with spoonful of syrup added to each bowl.

Endives and Chicken au Gratin

Serves 6 to 8

3 cups diced cooked chicken
8 firm young endives, about 1½ lb
2½ cups chicken broth
juice of ½ lemon
3 Tb butter
¼ cup flour
1 cup heavy cream
1 egg yolk
2 Tb grated Parmesan cheese
1 Tb bread crumbs

Preheat oven to 375 degrees.

Trim off the darkened ends of the endives, and cut into bite-size pieces. Put into pot with ½ cup of the chicken broth, the lemon juice, salt to taste if desired, and pepper. Cover, bring to a boil, and cook about 15 minutes, until the liquid has evaporated.

Meanwhile, melt butter in a saucepan, and add the flour, stirring. When blended, gradually add the remaining 2 cups of chicken broth, stirring well. Cook, stirring often, for about 10 minutes. Add the cream, plus salt and pepper, and continue cooking over low heat another 5 minutes, stirring often.

Add the chicken and two cups of the sauce to the endives. Stir to blend.

Add the egg yolk to the remaining sauce, and blend.

Spoon the chicken mixture into a baking dish.

Spoon remaining sauce over it, and sprinkle with the cheese and bread crumbs.

Bake in the oven 30 minutes, or until piping hot and golden brown on the top.

Serve over spaghetti if desired.

Belgian Endive

PLANTS WHICH START TO BLOOM IN FEBRUARY

Trees
Acacia sp. (most): yellow
Magnolia sp.: white to creamy, huge
(mid-Feb. to mid-March is the peak bloom)
Flowering Almond (*Prunus triloba*): pink
Flowering Plum (*Prunus blireiana*): pink
Cherry Plum (*Prunus cerasifera*): white

Shrubs
Boxleaf Azara (*Azara microphylla*): tiny yellow
blossoms are nearly invisible, but smell strongly
of vanilla or chocolate; lasts just two weeks
Forsythia (*F. intermedia*): yellow on bare branches
Leatherleaf Mahonia (*Mahonia bealei*): yellow,
along with blue-black fruit
Lily-of-the-Valley Shrub (*Pieris japonica*): white
urn-shaped
Chinese Pieris (*P. formosa forrestii*): white
urn-shaped
Spiraea (some species): white, pink, rose-red,
carmine

Ground Covers
Noell's Grevillea (*Grevillea* 'Noell'): white to rose
to pink
Pink Jasmine (*Jasminum polyanthum*): white to
pink and fragant
Fleabane (*Erigeron karvinskianus*): pink, fading
to white
Weeping Lantana (*Lantana montevidensis*):
lavender-magenta
Honey Bush (*Melianthes major*): red

Vines
Lilac Vine (*Hardenbergia comptoniana*): violet

Herbaceous/Woody Perennials
Purple Rock Cress (*Aubrieta deltoidea*): purple,
red, rose, or pale to deep lilac
Blister Cress (*Erysimum hieraciifolium*): yellow to
orange
Lenten Rose (*Hellebore orientalis*): lavender
Coral Bells/Alum Root (*Heuchera sanguinea*):
white, pink, green, crimson, reds on tall stalks
above leaves
Stock (*Matthiola incana*): many colors
Forget-Me-Not (*Myosotis sylvatica*): light blue
with yellow center

Annuals
Nemesia strumosa: yellow, orange, red, others
(bloom time can be from December to May,
depending on sowing time)
Sweet Pea (*Lathyrus odoratus*): many colors
Iceland Poppy (*Papaver nudicaule;* grown as an
annual here because our winters are too warm)

Bulbs
Anemone (*A. coronaria*): reds, white, or blues
Chasmanthe floribunda: red-orange
Crocus (*C. vernus*): yellows, oranges, blues,
lavenders
Dutch Hyacinth (*Hyacinthus orientalis*): fragrant
red, white, blue, or yellow
Spring Snowflake (*Leucojum aestivum*): white bell
with green dot on each petal tip
Grape Hyacinth (*Muscari armeniacum*): blue-purple
Also *M. botryoides*: blue

Natives
California Buckeye (*Aesculus californica*): starts to
leaf out
California Dutchman's Pipe Vine (*Aristolochia
californica*): creamy pipe-shaped
Ceanothus sp.: blue to violet to white
Leatherwood (*Dirca occidentalis*): lemon-yellow
(our unique East Bay native, hidden in our
remaining woodlands)
California Holly Grape (*Mahonia pinnata*): yellow
Pink-Flowering Currant (*Ribes sanguineum
glutinosum*): pink
Fuchsia-Flowered Gooseberry (*Ribes speciosum*):
crimson red, fuchsialike

Weeds
Bermuda Buttercup (*Oxalis pres-caprae*): deep
yellow

Magnolias

MARCH

Ah, spring! Although the weather is very variable this month and next and although westerly winds have intensified, bringing fog to our shoreline, inland areas and those up in the hills start to be a bit warmer, as the cold air from the ocean slides below a higher warm layer. March 20 is the Spring Equinox (the day when night and day are equal in length), and although other areas are still worrying about frost, in the East Bay warm weather is assured. Our plants certainly know it if we don't; the hills are bursting with color.

This is the best time of year to get up into the still-wild places and see our native wildflowers starting to bloom: **golden poppies, purple lupines, violet ceanothus, pink western redbud, manzanitas, summer holly,** and **Oregon grape.** Take at least one or two days out of your busy weekends and visit the U.C. Botanical Garden, the East Bay Regional Park District Botanical Garden, or the East Bay Regional Parks. On the way, you will also see a gorgeous show of bright yellow **broom** flowers all along the roadsides, where, unfortunately, they are taking the place of the natives that were disturbed by the road-building processes. But beware of **poison oak**; it is least visible right now.

Back in the cities, gardens are coming alive too. **Flowering cherry trees** burst into bloom, followed within a week by **flowering crabapples,** with their big red buds that open to reveal pink flowers. "Old" (not hybridized) **roses** begin to stir, along with **Mexican orange** (*Choisya ternata*), another old garden favorite, each sending its fragrance into the air (yes, roses used to smell). **Lilacs,** another East Coast favorite rarely seen here, join them. **Wild onions** have pushed their heads up in *every* moist shady corner, red-tipped **quince** shoots brighten the scene, and **wisteria** vines start to reawaken.

Many standard landscaping plants start to bloom in March and April: *Pittosporums,* **viburnums,** *Rhaphiolepis, Leptospermum,* **pyracanthas,** *Weigela.* Even your **California** (actually Chilean) **privet,** if not carefully sheared, will be covered with flowers. (Yes, you probably have one; it's that anonymous-looking hedge that was there before you moved in.) The plant with tall spikes of purple flowers is a Mediterranean transplant, **pride of Madeira** (*Echium fastuosum*) (it is also very obvious all over Marin County this month). The shrubs you see everywhere with bronzy-red new leaves are probably either **Australian brush cherry** (*Syzigium paniculatum*), **xylosma,** or **photinia.**

But enough looking! There's plenty of work to be done!

Pride of Madeira (Echium fastuosum)

PLANTING

March, during the dry spells, is the time to get the soil prepared for a summer garden. Turn under any green manure cover crops you planted last fall to add nitrogen to the soil. You can still add "hot" fertilizer (chicken or rabbit manure, bloodmeal) to your soil, so that it will be less hot by the time you plant (8 weeks before planting is optimum). Be careful, however, not to work the soil when it's soggy (see *September Planting*, p. 63 and *October Planting*, p. 69).

If your soil is already prepared (from last fall), you can take advantage of one of the special benefits of living in the East Bay: A spring crop of just about every **cool-season vegetable** noted in the *September Vegetable Planting* (p. 64) section can be grown to maturity before the hot weather affects them if planted now. However, this is your last chance to start some of them until fall. **Potatoes** planted around St. Patrick's Day are said to do well (no joke) and to mature by mid-June.

In addition, the more frost-tender leafy greens (**cilantro** and **parsley**) can now be planted. Cilantro (also called coriander) is especially critical to start now since it only does well in the mild periods between winter cold and summer heat.

All perennial vegetables and fruits can also be planted, including **artichokes** and **cardoons, asparagus, horseradish, rhubarb, caneberries (boysen, logan, olallie),** and **strawberries**; also edible flower crops, such as **borage, lovage,** and **angelica** (all perennials), **nasturtiums, shungiku/ edible chrysanthemum, calendula/pot marigold,** and **daylilies.**

March is also the first chance you have to start seeds (indoors in flats) of **warm-season crops,** which include most plants with edible fruits: **to-matoes, corn, eggplants, melons, okra, peppers,** and **peas** (including China or snow peas and sugar snap). (Yes, technically these are all "fruits," seed containers for the plant.) These plants are the "heat-lovers," and in the East Bay we should wait until April or May to put them into the ground; but if you're really eager to get a head start on a bumper crop this year, now's the time to do it. (Seeds of beans, cucumber, pumpkins, and summer squash, which are also warm-season fruit crops, should not, however, be started for about another month, and winter squash not until April 15.)

You may want to stagger your plantings, so that your vegetables ripen at different times. It's an especially good idea to stagger squash since in our East Bay foggy climate they invariably get powdery mildew, and it's nice to let the older plants go and have fresh ones coming along. It's also nice to select corn seed that will ripen early, midseason, and late so that you can have some throughout the summer. Be careful about tomatoes, eggplants, potatoes, strawberries, and peppers; if in past seasons your plants seemed to grow well, and then die before producing, your soil may carry **verticillium wilt.** You can buy resistant varieties of tomatoes; plenty of water in the dry autumn months will help all these plants fight the disease. If you've never planted these plants before, you may want to protect your other garden plants (olives, persimmon, avocado, pistachio, many stone fruits, xylosma, and many others; Japanese maples are especially susceptible) by planting the disease spreaders in pots or at least in a separate area of soil. Be sure not to dump soil from the pots back into the garden when you're done with the growing season! (although hot composting the used soil has been said to eliminate the disease pathogens). Also, be careful not to overwater your tomato seedlings when they're young; this can lead to blossom end rot later on.

March is also a fine time to get the rest of your garden growing. **Spring-** and **summer-flowering annuals** (see *May* through *August Bloom Lists*) and almost all **perennials** (except heat-lovers and sub-tropicals listed under *April, May,* and *June Planting*); **summer-flowering bulbs** you didn't plant in the fall; and **kitchen herbs** are all available at nurseries and can be planted now. Herbs from seeds can also be started. Trees, shrubs, and ground covers can also be planted, as long as the weather is typically cool and moist. In March and April, it's also okay to start grafting with scions collected last fall.

To conserve moisture and prevent weed growth, **mulching** is a good idea. Keep weeding!

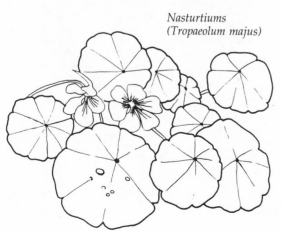

Nasturtiums (Tropaeolum majus)

FERTILIZING

Mature shrubs and trees need nitrogen with the start of their spring growth. (Exception: Cold-tender plants including the subtropicals noted above should not be fertilized yet.) This is also the time to fertilize the **cool-season lawn grasses** commonly grown here (bluegrass, fescue, bentgrass, and rye), which grow from March to May. You can reseed bare spots in your lawn, and you may need to start mowing. **Fuchsia** and **citrus** can be fertilized now, as new leaves appear.

PRUNING

Don't prune any of the "heavy bleeders" now (**maples, birches, elms**), as they are actively moving sugars stored in their roots up to their branches to produce this spring's leaves and will lose too much fluid if pruned now. Don't prune **ceanothus** (a native) until there is sure to be no more rain; if pruning is followed by rain, they are more susceptible to fungus dieback (*Sclerotinia fruticola*).

While they're still semidormant and have not yet started their summer growth, it's a prime time to divide **summer-** and **fall-flowering perennials** such as agapanthus, daylily, Shasta daisy, and yarrow.

INSECTS AND OTHER UNWELCOME GUESTS

The Chinese say that "insects awaken" in the early days of March. If you're a newcomer to California, **fleas** are probably driving you crazy, as they hatch from their over-wintering eggs. The Bay Area has been famous for its fleas since the time of the first Spanish explorers, who noted their presence with displeasure equal to yours. Luckily, long-term residents become tolerant of them, no longer having uncomfortable itchy reactions to their bites.

In the East Bay, we need to keep snail hunting and cleaning away snail hiding spots and also protect our seedling vegetables from the **birds**. A net cover may work, or try old tricks like a scarecrow or strips of white linen fluttering in the air. Covering the seeds with a thin layer of mulch works best.

HARVESTING

Collect volunteer seedlings/sprouts of young trees and shrubs from public parks before the mowing machines mow them down. March is also a prime time to collect all sorts of young **wild plant shoots** for greens. New young leaves of **dandelions, nettles, dock, filaree, alum root, mallow, plantain,** and **prickly lettuce** can be added to soups, some even to salads; **chickweed, sheep sorrel, miner's lettuce, shepherd's purse, sow thistle, mint, mustard, nasturtium, purslane, watercress,** and **lambsquarter** are good in raw salads. Use only a small portion of the stronger-tasting ones.

Valencia oranges are in season from March and April until June, or even November.

California Poppy and Douglas Iris

MARCH EVENTS

Dahlia Root Sale—Dahlia Society of California (Golden Gate Park Hall of Flowers), and San Leandro Dahlia Society

Ikebana International Flower Show—call Lakeside Park Visitor Center for information on location

Pruning Demonstration—Strybing Arboretum, Golden Gate Park

Fuji Bonsai Club—Lakeside Park, Oakland

Wild Flower Show—Golden Gate Park Hall of Flowers

Pacific Regional Daffodil Show—Lakeside Park, Oakland

San Francisco Orchid Society Show—Golden Gate Park Hall of Flowers

Mountain View Cemetery: 35,000 tulips in bloom, late March into April, just inside entrance—5000 Piedmont Avenue, Oakland

If the winter was wet and mild, this may be a good year for desert wildflowers. The best place to see them in great numbers is the deserts of Southern California around Lancaster and Palmdale. The Automobile Association usually has up-to-date information on where to see them.

RECIPES

Broccoli Soup with Buttermilk

Serves 4 to 6

It will soon be time to pull the last of your winter-crop broccoli and potatoes out of the ground to make room for spring crops; they may be starting to go to seed anyway. So feast on the last of the crop with this hearty dinner soup. (Other leafy greens going to seed now should also be tasty cooked this way.)

1 or 2 bunches fresh broccoli, about 1 ¾ lb, cut into bite-size pieces
2 potatoes, about ¾ lb, cut to bite-size
2 Tb butter
½–1 cup finely chopped onions
1 tsp finely minced or mashed garlic
1 can chicken broth + ½ can water
1 cup buttermilk
½ tsp (no more!) nutmeg
¼ tsp cayenne pepper
½ cup finely chopped fresh dill
salt and pepper to taste, if desired

Melt butter in a large pot and sauté the onions and garlic; when these are soft, add the potatoes and then the broccoli. (You may want to reserve a few broccoli flowerets for garnish; they may be parboiled.)

Add the chicken broth and water, bring to a boil, and simmer about 20 minutes or until the potatoes are cooked.

Ladle the mixture in small portions into an electric blender and blend thoroughly.

Return to the pot, and add the buttermilk, nutmeg, and cayenne. Add the broccoli flowerets and serve, sprinkled with the dill.

Pennsylvania Dutch Wilted Dandelion Salad

Serves 4

1 lb young dandelion leaves
Dressing:
1 tsp butter
¾ cup sour cream
1 egg, well beaten
2 tsp sugar
1 Tb vinegar
½ tsp salt
¼ tsp pepper

Wash, drain well, and tear dandelion leaves into bite-size pieces.

Melt butter. Combine rest of ingredients and add to butter, stirring until dressing thickens and comes to a boil. Pour over greens immediately, toss, and serve.

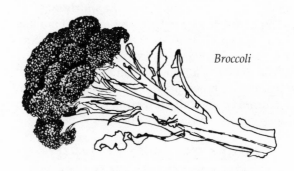

Broccoli

PLANTS WHICH START TO BLOOM IN MARCH

Trees

Knife Acacia (*Acacia cultriformis*): yellow
Blackwood Acacia (*Acacia melanoxylon*): cream
European White Birch (*Betula pendula*): catkins
Flowering Dogwood (*Cornus florida*): creamy
  white on bare branches
Bronze Loquat (*Eriobotrya deflexa*): creamy white,
  and green new growth
Coral Gum (*Eucalyptus torquata*): coral red and
  yellow
Flowering Crabapple (*Malus floribunda*): red buds,
  then gorgeous pink flowers on bare branches
Saucer Magnolia (*Magnolia soulangiana*):
  stupendous big white blooms on bare branches
  (early March especially)
Japanese Flowering Cherry (*Prunus serrulata*):
  white to pink on bare branches

Shrubs

Glossy Abelia (*A. grandiflora*): white
Mexican Orange (*Choisya ternata*): white and
  fragrant
Irish and Scotch Brooms (*Cytisus* sp.): golden yellow
Pride of Madeira (*Echium fastuosum*): spikes of
  blue-purple
Gamolepis chrysanthemoides: yellow daisylike
  (looks almost exactly like *Euryops pectinatus*,
  but blooms now)
Rose-of-Sharon (*Hibiscus syriacus*): many colors
California Privet (*Ligustrum ovalifolium*): white
Osmanthus delavayi: white and fragrant
Chinese Photinia (*Photinia serrulata*): dramatic
  white, with bright red bronzy new growth
Chinese Pieris (*Pieris formosa forrestii*): white bells,
  with scarlet new growth
Lily-of-the-Valley Shrub (*Pieris japonica*): white bells
Japanese Mock Orange/Australian Laurel
  (*Pittosporum tobira*): white and yellow and fragrant
Indian Hawthorn (*Rhaphiolepis indica*): white
  (actually throughout much of the year, but
  most prolific now)
Australian Brush Cherry (*Syzigium paniculatum*):
  bronzy new growth
Tamarix parviflora: showy pink
Viburnum burkwoodii: white
Xylosma congestum: bronzy new growth

Ground Covers

Woolly Grevillea (*Grevillea lanigera*): white to rose
  to red

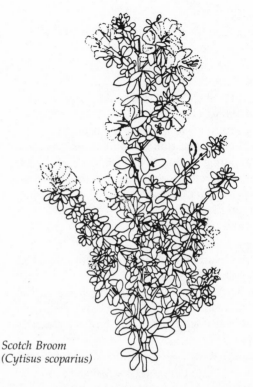

Scotch Broom
(Cytisus scoparius)

Sea Pink (*Armeria maritima*): pink
Serbian Bellflower (*Campanula poscharskyana*):
  violet to blue
Hottentot Fig (*Carpobrotus edulis*): yellow
Kenilworth Ivy (*Cymbalaria muralis*): blue violet
Trailing Gazania (*Gazania rigens leucantha*): yellow
Lavender Starflower (*Grewia occidentalis*): lavender
Trailing Ice Plant (*Lampranthus spectablis*): purple
Blue Star Creeper (*Laurentia fluviatilis*): light blue
Common Periwinkle (*Vinca minor*): violet

Vines

Fiveleaf Akebia (*Akebia quinata*): purple rose
Evergreen Clematis (*Clematis armandii*): white
Carolina Jessamine (*Gelsemium sempervirens*):
  yellow

Herbaceous/Woody Perennials

African Daisy (*Arctotis* sp.): yellow to orange with
  dark centers (+ white, pink, red, purplish,
  cream, orange cvs.)
Marguerite (*Chrysanthemum frutescens*): white,
  yellow, pink
Bleeding Heart (*Dicentra spectabilis*): rose and white
Blanket Flower (*Gaillardia x grandiflora*): red with
  yellow tips
Geum quellyon/G. chiloense: orange to red, on
  stalks above leaves
Heliotrope (*Heliotropium arborescens*): violet

Annuals

African Daisy (*Dimorphotheca*): cream to gold
Baby Blue Eyes (*Nemophila*): blue
Tulip (*Tulipa* hybrids): many colors

Bulbs

Spanish Bluebell/Squill (*Endymion hispanicus*):
   blue, white, pink, or purple bell
Hippeastrum: white, pink, or red trumpet
Spring Star Flower (*Ipheion uniflorum*): white to
   deep purple + purple midvein on each petal
Persian Buttercup (*Ranunculus asiaticus*): yellow,
   orange, scarlet, crimson, pink, white, bicolors
Harlequin Flower (*Sparaxis tricolor*): yellow +
   burgundy + red tips

Natives

Western Columbine (*Aquilegia formosa*): orange,
   red, yellow, or bicolored
Manzanitas and Bearberry (*Arctostaphylos* sp.): white
   to pink bells
Sea Fig/Native Ice Plant (*Carpobrotus chilensis*):
   purple
Western Redbud (*Cercis occidentalis*): profuse red to
   rose, fading to pink, on bare branches
Summer Holly (*Comarostaphylis diversifolia*): white
Western Bleeding Heart (*Dicentra formosa*): pink
   to rose "bleeding hearts"
California Poppy (*Eschscholzia californica*): golden
Southern Flannel Bush (*Fremontodendron
   mexicanum*): yellow to orange
Douglas Iris (*Iris douglasiana*): deep red-purple
   (+ white, cream, yellow, blue-violet varieties)
Tidy Tips (*Layia platyglossum*): yellow with white tips
Prickly Phlox (*Leptodactylon californicum*): pink
Lupines (*Lupinus* sp.): blue-violet
Oregon Grape (*Mahonia aquifolium*): yellow
Nevin Mahonia (*Mahonia nevinii*): yellow
Blue-Eyed Grass (*Sisyrinchium bellum*): blue-purple
Huckleberry (*Vaccinium ovatum*): white waxy bell

Weeds

Wild Onion (*Allium triquetrum*): white drooping bells
Scarlet Pimpernel (*Anagallis arvensis*): salmon
Wild Mustard (*Brassica nigra, B. campestris*): yellow
White-Stemmed Filaree/Storksbill (*Erodium
   moschatum*): pinkish
Cranesbill/Wild Geranium (*Geranium carolinianum*):
   pinkish
Wild Radish (*Raphanus sativus*): white to pinkish

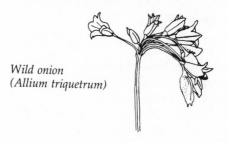

*Wild onion
(Allium triquetrum)*

APRIL

It's warmer, though foggy, and with a few last showers. In the hills you might see natives like **bush poppy, ceanothus, dogwood, flannel bush, lupine, manzanita, redbud, buttonwillows, ninebark, longleaf mahonia,** and *Dianthus formosa* in bloom. April is usually the month of the **native wildflower show** put on by the California Native Plant Society at the Oakland Museum.

Fruit trees have all leafed out, accompanied by the first tinkling of ice cream trucks. Natives are joined in bloom by many more of the exotics we have brought to this area. Some of our deciduous plants that need warmer weather to get going, such as the **silk tree** (*Albizia julibrissin*) and the **jacaranda,** finally leaf out in very late April. It is a month for **flower shows**; check events at Lakeside Park and Strybing. Also visit U.C. Botanical Garden, Dunsmuir House in Oakland, and (on weekdays only) the Blake Estate in Kensington.

By mid-April, **wisteria** vines all over the East Bay come into full bloom. The **native azaleas** and **rhododendrons** are starting their show all along California's north coast; if you can't get up to see them (Krause State Rhododendron Reserve in Mendocino is one place), you can console yourself at the McLaren Rhododendron Dell at Strybing Arboretum in Golden Gate Park, at the U.C. Botanical Garden, or at Lakeside Park in Oakland.

PLANTING AND FERTILIZING

If you live in a fairly warm microclimate and if the East Bay is having a not unusually cold spring, by mid- to late-April you might be able to start setting out seedlings of the summer-season vegetables and annuals you started in March. It's also time to sow seeds of annual herbs (until July 15), such as **anise,** the **basils, German chamomile, caraway, chervil, cumin, dill,** and **summer savory**; and perennial herbs (until August), including **bee balm/bergamot** (*Monarda* sp.), **borage, Roman chamomile, catnip, chives, garlic chives (gow choy), lavender, marjoram, mint** (be careful—very invasive!), **oregano, pennyroyal, rosemary, rue, sage, French sorrel** (also invasive), **tarragon,** and **thyme.** It should also still be cool and moist enough to plant trees, shrubs, ground covers, and perennials.

In April, the more "tender" (harmed by cold) plants we grow can be planted: subtropicals such as **avocado, bougainvillea, citrus, fuchsia, guava, hibiscus, lantana,** and **princess flower/pleroma/ tibouchina. Citrus** can also be safely pruned now. It's a good time to take **softwood cuttings** of trees and shrubs and tip cuttings of herbaceous perennials.

Now is also the time to sow seeds in flats indoors of **beans, cucumbers, summer squash,** and **pumpkins**; **winter squash** is okay to sow after mid-

*Red Valerian
(Centranthus ruber)*

April. If you think you've got a warm enough miniclimate to try growing them, **melons** can also be started now. A number of **cooler-season crops** can still be planted outdoors, including green onions, bulbing onions, and parsley, chard, chives, kohlrabi, leek, and cos lettuces (this is about the last time you should be starting these until next fall); Brussels sprouts, endive and parsnips may be started from now through July, and beets, cabbages, carrots, leaf lettuces, radishes, and potatoes (seed-eyes) (actually a warm-season crop traditionally because it is not frost-hardy, but listed here because it is also not really a heat-lover) may be started from now through August. (Again, there are places in the East Bay were many of these can be started nearly year-round. The risk is that they will "bolt" (go to seed) if you are in too warm a microclimate, or if we get extra-warm weather.)

Fertilize roses, shrubs, and anything else you haven't yet. Keep composting (the weed explosion going on in your garden should give you ample material) and adding organic material, i.e., from your compost pile, to the soil or using it for mulch (a top layer to keep the soil moist and covered).

Tend to plants already started, and don't let newly planted plants dry out, not even for half a day. Watch for signs of temporary wilt to let you know which plants need more water.

Spring-flowering bulbs need to be cared for even after they finish blooming; keeping their foliage green and growing by continuing to water them will produce a nice bloom next year.

If you're growing **California poppies,** watering them now can greatly extend their bloom.

INSECTS AND DISEASES

Aphid predators search out high-protein, high-sugar foods to sustain them during their search for aphids. If your garden does not have enough flowers in bloom now (especially *Umbellifers* and *Composites* with their small flowers and nectar and pollen within easy reach) to invite aphid predators to stay, you may be getting an **aphid** invasion on some plants, especially those high in nitrogen. You can rinse them off with a strong jet of water, or you can let them go to attract predators that will be arriving later in the spring. Be careful not to harm **ladybug larvae,** which don't look at all like the adults but which are also voracious aphid eaters. If you use chemical insecticides, try not to spray now; these and many other beneficial insects are hatching.

Hope for dry days because a wet period in April and May can encourage many disease organisms to flourish later in the season: botrytis in petunias and marigolds, petal blight in camellias and azaleas, brown rot of stone fruits, peach leaf curl, and anthracnose in sycamores (the disease that causes London plane trees to lose so many of their leaves in spring).

Also, as soon as they've bloomed, start checking for signs of **fireblight** in some plants of the pome tribe of the rose family. This looks like a browning (as if the plant has been burned) that starts at the flowers and moves down the stalk. Prune as soon as noticed, to prevent spreading which could kill the whole plant. Susceptible plants include the pyracantha, quince (both flowering and fruiting), loquat, pear, toyon, mountain ash (*Sorbus*), hawthorn, photinia, apple, and crabapple.

HARVESTING

Revel in **asparagus!** Harvest and eat all **cool-season vegetables** from last fall's planting before they go to seed. You may want to let some of them set seeds for next year's planting, unless they're from hybridized varieties, in which case they won't breed true. In mid-April, Guatemalan **Hass avocados** become available (through July, or even November). **Fava beans** ripen April through June.

APRIL EVENTS

Rare and Choice Plant Sale—Strybing Arboriculture Society, Golden Gate Park Hall of Flowers

East Bay Dahlia Society Root Sale—Lakeside Park, Oakland

Classes in Sogetsu Ikebana flower arranging—Oakland Parks and Recreation Department

California Spring Blossom and Wildflower Association—Golden Gate Park Hall of Flowers

American Rhododendron Society Show—Lakeside Park, Oakland

California Spring Garden Show—Lakeside Park, Oakland

Native Plants Sale—Tilden Botanical Garden, Berkeley

Native Plant Society Wildflower Show—Oakland Museum (sometimes held in May)

RECIPES

Fava Bean Spaghetti/Ful

Serves 4

If you planted favas as a ground cover last fall, they should be bearing their pods now. Dried fava beans need hours of soaking, but fresh ones, right from the garden, are quick to prepare. The outer pod is not eaten; return it to your compost pile for a gift of nitrogen.

Favas are not a well-known food in the United States (outside of Italian communities), but they are a staple for much of North Africa and the Mediterranean. In Spain, soups are made with them. In Egypt, they are eaten nearly daily, in a delicious national dish called "Ful" or "Ful Medames." This recipe is basically the Egyptian dish but served over a plate of spaghetti, with cheese as an optional garnish. Deelish!

fava beans, about 2 cups
½–1 onion (red or white), finely chopped
olive oil to cover bottom of cooking pan
juice of a lemon
garlic, minced or mashed, to taste
cumin and salt to taste
2–4 hard-boiled eggs
spaghetti
parsley
Parmesan or Romano cheese, grated

Simmer the fava beans and onions in olive oil over a low flame until the beans are soft, adding water as they start to stick, and continue cooking a half-hour to an hour. When you can mash them with a fork, you have the option of breaking them up to make more of a pasty sauce (with a fork or in a blender) or leaving them whole. Either way, add the lemon juice, garlic, cumin, and salt. Allow this to simmer while you cook the spaghetti.

Serve over spaghetti, garnished with bite-size pieces of hard-boiled egg, chopped parsley (optional), and grated Parmesan or Romano cheese (optional).

Asparagus

Vietnamese Crab-Asparagus Soup

Serves 4

2 shallots (or white part of green onion)
4 oz crab meat
1 Tb peanut (or other vegetable) oil
1 lb asparagus spears
1½ cups chicken broth (14 oz can)
1 cup water
1 Tb cornstarch
1 egg
dash black pepper
lemon or lime

Slice shallots in thin rounds and flake crab meat. Heat oil and sauté crab meat and shallots on high heat for 1 minute, stirring constantly.

Add asparagus and stir briskly about 1 minute, shredding the asparagus. Add chicken broth and water, stir well, bring to a boil, and cook on a high heat 2 minutes.

Mix cornstarch with some of the hot soup liquid in a cup until smooth (to prevent lumpiness). Add to soup and stir well. Bring to a boil, and cook 1 or 2 minutes until slightly thickened.

Beat egg lightly, then add to soup, stirring immediately with a circular motion around the pot, to make strings of cooked egg. Sprinkle with pepper.

Serve hot with large slices of lemon or lime, and more black pepper for seasoning the soup to taste.

PLANTS WHICH START TO BLOOM IN APRIL

Trees
Australian Tea Tree (*Leptospermum laevigatum*): white or pink

Shrubs
Lemon Bottlebrush (*Callistemon citrinus*): red bottlebrush
Breath-of-Heaven (*Coleonema album, C. pulchrum*): white, pink
Fraser's Photinia (*Photinia fraseri*): white
Karo (*Pittosporum crassifolium*): maroon/purple and fragrant
Tawhiwhi (*Pittosporum tenuifolium*): teeny purplish/maroon but fragrant (especially at night)

Victorian Box (*Pittosporum undulatum*):
  creamy white and fragrant
Pomegranate (*Punica granatum*): orange red, cream
Pyracantha: white
"Old" (not hybridized) Roses (*Rosa* sp.): many colors
Australian Brush Cherry (*Syzigium paniculatum*):
  white (sometimes called by its old name *Eugenia*)
Common Snowball (*Viburnum opulus* 'Roseum'):
  white
Leatherleaf Viburnum (*Viburnum rhytidophyllum*):
  white
Sandankwa Viburnum (*Viburnum suspensum*): white
Weigela florida: pink to rose red

Ground Covers

Woolly Yarrow (*Achillea tomentosa*): yellow
Carpet Bugle (*Ajuga reptans*): blue to purple
Snow-in-Summer (*Cerastium tomentosum*): white
Rock Cotoneaster (*Cotoneaster horizontalis*):
  white to pink
Rosea Ice Plant (*Drosanthemum floribundum*):
  rose to pink
Blister Cress (*Erysimum kotschyanum*): yellow
Ground Cover Geranium (*Geranium incanum*):
  purple to magenta
Blue Marguerite (*Felicia amelloides*): blue
Sunrose (*Helianthemum nummularium*): white or
  yellow or orange or red or rose-pink
Hypericum coris: yellow
Lady Bank's Rose (*Rosa banksiae*): white, yellow
Creeping Speedwell (*Veronica repens*): violet

Vines

Chinese and Japanese Wisteria (*Wisteria sinensis,
  W. floribunda*): violet (+ white, pink cvs.)
"Invader"/'Himalaya' Blackberry (*Rubus procerus*):
  white

Herbaceous/Woody Perennials

Columbine (*Aquilegia*): blue or yellow + cvs.
Basket of God (*Aurinia saxatilis*): golden yellow
Bedding Begonia (*B. semperflorens-cultorum*):
  white to pink to red
Slipper Flower (*Calceolaria crenatiflora*): yellow,
  red, orange + markings
Cosmos bipinnatus: white + pinks, roses,
  lavenders, purples, crimsons with yellow centers
Chinese Forget-Me-Not (*Cynoglossum amabile*):
  light blue
Perennial Candytuft (*Iberis sempervirens*): white
Crown-Pink (*Lychnis coronaria*): cerise, white,
  crimson + cvs.
Cup Flower (*Nierembergia* sp.): violet-blue to
  lavender

Annuals

Snapdragon (*Antirrhinum majus*): many colors
  (grown as an annual due to Rust)
Wallflower (*Cheiranthus cheiri*): many colors
Sweet William (*Dianthus barbatus*): fragrant white,
  pink, red, or blue
Carnation (*Dianthus caryophyllus*): many colors
  (grown as an annual due to Rust)
Chinese Pinks (*D. chinensis*): many colors
Baby Snapdragon/Toadflax (*Linaria maroccana*):
  red, gold, rose, pink, mauve, chamois, blue,
  violet, or purple
Love-in-a-Mist (*Nigella damascena*): blue, white, rose
Verbena: fragrant purple, white, pink, red, blue,
  bicolors (grown as an annual because our
  winters are too mild)

Bulbs

Montbretia (*Crocosmia x crocosmiflora*): red-orange
Freesia: many colors
Iris (Dutch and Bearded): many colors
Star of Bethlehem (*Ornithogalum umbellatum*):
  white with green stripe outside each petal

Natives

Mountain Mahogany (*Cercocarpus betuloides*):
  white, fragrant
Pacific Dogwood (*Cornus nuttallii*): white saucers
  on nearly-bare branches
Bush Poppy (*Dendromecon rigida*): yellow
Beach Strawberry (*Fragaria chiloensis*): white
Flannel Bush (*Fremontodendron californicum*):
  yellow (plus orange fading blossoms at the
  same time)
Ocean Spray (*Holodiscus discolor*): white plumes
Longleaf Mahonia (*Mahonia nervosa*): yellow
Ninebark (*Physocarpus capitatus*): white
Western Azalea (*Rhododendron occidentale*):
  white to pink, on bare branches, and
  fragrant (+ yellow, orange, red cvs.)
Thimbleberry (*Rubus parviflorus*): white
Native Blackberry (*Rubus vitifolius*): white

*Golden Columbine
(Aquilegia chrysantha)*

MAY

May is the beginning of the dry season in the East Bay. Rarely will it rain past the beginning of the month. Grasses dry up and go to seed; trees bear pollen, making this the worst month for allergy sufferers (especially on breezy days).

On the other hand, the warm weather also encourages warmer weather plants to blossom, and some of our most dramatic bloomers get going this month: **gardenias, catalpas, jacarandas, yesterday-today-tomorrow.** Be sure to catch the show at the U.C. Botanical Garden when the blue-violet **empress tree** comes into bloom; or visit Strybing Botanical Garden in Golden Gate Park for the yellow waterfall of the **goldenrain tree.** Take a walk on a warm night and smell the **mock oranges, sweetshade, guavas, gardenias, star jasmine,** and **night-scented stock.** The **Portuguese laurel** used in many gardens as an informal shrub is covered with creamy white flowers, and the **hawthorn trees** brought from England and Europe have a show of white which will become rose-red in the fall. That other English favorite, the **horse chestnut,** is covered with pink, then red, then white blooms. In the hills, our native chestnut, the **buckeye,** is also in bloom, along with the **bush anemone, coral bells, blue elderberry, penstemon,** and **St. Catherine's lace.** And in our yards (probably where you don't want it) invader **Himalaya blackberry** (*Rubus procerus*) is taking over, even though it looks almost forgivable at this time of year, covered with white blossoms and attended by bees.

May is the other big month for flower shows, including **azaleas** and **rhododendrons, African violets, orchids,** and **iris.** This is the month to visit the Berkeley Municipal Rose Garden, the Oakland Rose Garden, and the Golden Gate Park Rose Garden in San Francisco.

May 4 is the start of the summer season, and active hummingbirds attest to the fact that the earth is fully waking up.

WATERING

Now that the rains are over, we have to take over with our garden hose, that is, unless you've planted your garden with drought-tolerant natives or Mediterranean-climate plants. You may need to start deep-watering some nonnative trees and shrubs once or twice a month: Build basins around them. This is a rest period for natives though; *don't* water them.

Annual bluegrass, as well as other bluegrasses, bentgrass, fescue, and ryegrasses, all **"cool-season" lawn** grasses, start to go brown now. You should keep watering to keep the roots alive, but don't fertilize or mow. The compost pile may also need to be wetted occasionally.

PLANTING

After May 1 you can definitely set out all warm-season vegetable seedlings, as well as summer-flowering annuals. This is also a good time to plant **strawberry** and **citrus** and set out seedlings of **beans, cucumbers, pumpkins, squash,** and **melons. Amaranth**, sometimes thought of as "summer spinach," and **New Zealand spinach** (popular as a warm-weather spinach substitute crop) are also good to plant now. Also, **softwood cuttings** are still okay, as well as **tip-cuttings** of any herbaceous plant. **Dahlia** bulbs are now available at the nurseries.

Chives

45

Seeds of **heat-loving annuals** may now be sown, including ***Ageratum, Calliopsis/Coreopsis, Celosia,* gloriosa daisy** (*Rudbeckia hurta*), **madagascar periwinkle** (*Vinca rosea*), **annual phlox, marigold, petunia, salpiglossis, verbena, zinnia.** If you want to grow **money plant** (*Lunaria*), now is a good time to sow seeds; the silver seed pods won't develop until late summer to fall, but the plant needs a long warm period to mature and ripen its pods.

PRUNING

After the growth flush of spring slows, it's a good time for pruning, especially of plants that bloom on "old" wood, that is, those that already have blossomed. It's also time to start controlling some of the rampant growth that's taking place in your garden. Pinch **azaleas, fuchsias, geraniums, impatiens,** and **marguerites** if you want them to grow bushier. If it's necessary, now is the time to prune older **citrus** (until midsummer). Remove suckers that grow from grafted roses and fruit trees. Remove faded **iris** flowers and stalks (though not healthy leaves). Cut and enjoy flowers; Mother's Day, oddly enough, comes right in the middle of this month. Cutting roses and other blooms for indoor decoration will encourage a second batch of blooms.

MAINTENANCE

Fertilize and mulch **azaleas, rhododendrons,** and **camellias** after they've bloomed, and continue to fertilize other plants. While you're doing this, start "dead-heading" the first group of plants (cutting off dead flowers) and cleaning carefully around the area to prevent camellia petal blight fungus from being carried over to the next growing season. **Roses** may get mildew, rust, or black spot around this time. Use an **earwig** trap (paper towel tube or rolled newspaper) if they seem to be unduly bothering your seedling vegetables (said to happen mostly near eucalyptus trees, though no one knows why). Earwigs will enter the trap during the daylight hours because it provides a dark hiding place; they can then be burned. **Houseplant cyclamens** need to be put outside to get the nighttime cool; and, in fact, most houseplants can be put outside (in indirect sunlight) to enjoy the warm weather. Protect transplants from hot spells with a shade cloth if necessary. Keep mulching; it will help keep the soil moist during these ever-warmer days.

HARVESTING

If you planted early (February/March), you may already be starting to be able to harvest cool-season crops. When your **potatoes** start flowering, you can start digging up individual "new potatoes" (small but very tasty), leaving the rest of the plant in the ground until you're ready to harvest more. **Lisbon** and **Eureka lemons** fruit all year in the East Bay, but most heavily in the spring. May to June is the year's first season for **figs** (grown on "old" wood, the branches produced last year). Locally grown **strawberries** become available at the market from May 1 until mid-October. (If you have a strawberry-looking ground cover in your yard, but with bland, hard fruit, it may be mock strawberry [*Duchesnea indica*].)

Tropical fruits begin to show up in the market. The peak season for **mango** runs from May to August. **Marsh** and **Ruby Pink Grapefruits,** unlike other citrus which fruit mostly in the winter months, are available from May to September/October. The **kiwis** in the market, however, from now until October, are from New Zealand. **Bananas** fruit from May to September or later. (Though usually not grown in the East Bay, it is said that they fruit quite well if grown in a greenhouse or indoors. Lakeside Park Gardens has several banana plants that fruit.)

MAY EVENTS

Sydney B. Mitchell Iris Society Show—Lakeside Park, Oakland

American Rhododendron Show—Golden Gate Park Hall of Flowers

California Spring Garden Show—Dunsmuir House, Oakland

African Violet Society of San Francisco—Golden Gate Hall Park Hall of Flowers

East Bay African Violet Society—Lakeside Park, Oakland

San Francisco Rose Society—Golden Gate Park Hall of Flowers

Berkeley Municipal Rose Garden—Euclid Avenue at Bayview Place

Oakland Rose Garden (Morcom Amphitheater of Roses)—Jean and Olive Streets (special event on Mother's Day)

Golden Gate Park Rose Garden—San Francisco

Old Garden Rose Section, Heritage Roses—Albany Community Center

RECIPES

Feta Pasta and Avocado Cream Soup

Serves 4

The last of your green onions are probably harvestable now; also the last of the crop of Fuerte avocados is in the stores, and the Hass is at its height of season. So here's a set of recipes to use them both with the fanfare they deserve, along with lemons from your tree. A wonderful, early summer dinner.

Feta Pasta

6 oz Japanese somen (thin) noodles, or 12 oz egg
   noodles
8 oz Greek or Italian feta cheese
3 Tb fresh lemon juice
4 garlic cloves, pressed
1 cup olive oil
2 Tb wine vinegar
1 Tb pepper
1 cup dry white wine
½ cup fresh orange juice
8 green onions, chopped
2 oranges, peeled and sectioned

Combine all ingredients except noodles in a blender and puree. Cook noodles in about 3 quarts of water. Pour puree over, mix, and serve.

Sopa de Aguacate/Avocado Cream Soup

2 avocados, peeled
¾ cup sour cream or heavy cream
3 cups chicken broth (or 15 oz can + 1 cup water)
¼ cup dry sherry
½ tsp pepper
1 or 2 tortillas, quartered and fried until crisp

Puree the avocados and cream in a blender. Bring broth to a boil, reduce to a simmer, and stir in avocado puree. Add sherry and pepper.

Top with tortilla pieces or avocado slices. Serve warm, or refrigerate until cold.

Heavenly Spinach Salad

Serves 4 to 6

A wonderful treat to make with your early spring crop.

½ bunch spinach
2 oranges
½ red onion
Dressing:
¼ cup olive oil
¼ cup red wine vinegar
1 Tb honey
6 leaves basil, minced
½ lemon
¼ tsp salt
½ tsp mayonnaise (emulsifies the oil and vinegar)
1 or more slices bacon, crumbled
Garnish:
walnut bits (for a real treat, smoked or grilled)

Cut or tear spinach and slice oranges and red onion into bite-size pieces.

Prepare dressing by combining all ingredients, dress salad, and serve with garnish.

Avocado and Lemon

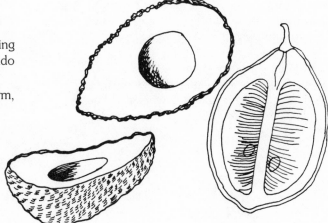

PLANTS WHICH START TO BLOOM IN MAY AND JUNE

*California Buck-Eye
(Aesculus californica)*

Trees

Horse Chestnut (*Aesculus carnea*): pink to red, fading to white

Bottle Tree (*Brachychiton populneus*): white bottlebrush

Catalpa (*Catalpa bignonioides*): white

Evergreen Dogwood (*Cornus capitata*): pale yellow to white bracts

English Hawthorn (*Crataegus laevigata*): white

Red-Flowering Gum (*Eucalyptus ficifolia*): light red, cream, light pink, salmon, orange

Silk Oak (*Grevillea robusta*): orange to yellow

Sweetshade (*Hymenosporum flavum*): yellow and fragrant

Jacaranda mimosifolia: showy lavender-blue

Laburnum watereri: spectacular cascades of yellow

Cow Itch (*Lagunaria patersonii*): showy pink

Southern Magnolia (*Magnolia grandiflora*): white

Empress Tree (*Paulownia tomentosa*): spectacular cascades of blue-violet (Be sure not to miss seeing the one at U.C. Botanical Garden.)

Shrubs

Flowering Maple (*Abutilon* sp.): white, yellow, pink, or red, pale orange

Yesterday-Today-Tomorrow (*Brunfelsia pauciflora* 'Floribunda'): purple, then lavender, then white

Weeping Bottlebrush (*Callistemon viminalis*): red bottlebrush

Rockroses (*Cistus* sp.): white, pinks, often with contrasting spot

Bush Morning Glory (*Convolvulus cneorum*): white

Cotoneaster sp.: white

Canary Bird Bush (*Crotolaria agatiflora*): yellow-green

Cigar Plant (*Cuphea ignea*): red

Guava (*Feijoa sellowiana*): red bottlebrushes

Gardenia (*Gardenia augusta*): white and fragrant

Purple Tobacco (*Iochroma cyaneum*): violet

Blue Solanum (*Lycianthes rantonnetii*): lavender

Oleander (*Nerium oleander*): many colors

Mock Orange (*Philadelphus coronarius*): white and fragrant

Diamond-Leaf Pittosporum (*Pittosporum rhombifolium*): white and fragrant (at the same time as orange fruit)

Portuguese Laurel (*Prunus lusitanica*): creamy white

Salvia greggii: red

Ground Covers

Dwarf Coreopsis (*Coreopsis auriculata* 'Nana'): yellow

Crane's Bill (*Erodium chamaedryoides*): white

Sweet Woodruff (*Galium odoratum*): white on tall stalks above foliage

Spanish Shawl (*Heterocentron elegans*): magenta

Lippia (*Phyla nodiflora*): pink + red + purple + white

Spring Cinquefoil (*Potentilla tabernaemontanii*): yellow

Red Ground Cover Verbena (*Verbena peruviana*): red

Australian Violet (*Viola hederacea*): violet

Vines

Star Jasmine (*Trachelospermum jasminoides*): white and fragrant

*Purple Tobacco
(Iochroma cyaneum)*

*Sea Lavender
(Limonium perezii)*

Herbaceous Perennials

Yarrow (*Achillea* sp.): white, yellow, cream
Hollyhock (*Alcea rosea/Althea rosea*): many colors
Peruvian Lily (*Alstroemeria aurantiaca*): many
  colors (mid-June)
Aster sp.: many colors
Meadow Sweet (*Astilbe sp.*): white, pink, or
  red plumes
Shasta Daisy (*Chrysanthemum maximum*): white
  with yellow center
Dusty Miller (*Centauria cineraria*): yellow or purple
Coreopsis: yellow, orange, maroon, or reddish
Larkspur (*Delphinium elatum*): blue outside, dark
  purple inside
Fortnight Lily (*Dietes vegeta*): white + yellow
  + brown-purple
Foxglove (*Digitalis purpurea*): purple, pink, white,
  or yellow
Baby's Breath (*Gypsophila paniculata*): tiny white
Strawflower (*Helichrysum bracteatum*): many colors
Plantain Lily (*Hosta* sp.): white, lavender, blue
Impatiens: many colors
Red Hot Poker Plant (*Kniphofia uvaria*):
  red-orange, yellow
Sea Lavender (*Limonium perezii*): blue-violet
  + white
Statice (*Limonium sinuatum*): many colors
Lobelia (*L. erinus*): blue-violet
Flowering Tobacco (*Nicotiana alata*): red!
Water Lilies (*Nymphaea* sp.): many colors
Penstemon (*P. gloxinoides*): many colors
Petunia: many colors
Balloon Flower (*Platycodon grandiflorus*): violet,
  white or pink, with yellow centers
Pincushion Flower (*Scabiosa caucasica*): powder
  blue, purple, or white

Annuals

Flossflower (*Ageratum houstonianum*): lavender,
  pinks, white
Cockscomb (*Celosia argentea*): many colors
Bachelor's Button/Cornflower (*Centaurea cyanus*):
  many colors
Globe Candytuft (*Iberis umbellata*): white, purple,
  violet, red
Night-Scented Stock (*Matthiola longipetala*): purple
Oriental Poppy (*Papaver orientale*): many colors
Painted Tongue (*Salpiglossis sinuata*): mahogany
  red, red-orange, yellow, purple, or pink shades
Mealy-Cup Sage 'Victoria' and 'Blue Bedder'
  (*Salvia farinacea*): blue purple
Scarlet Sage (*Salvia splendens*): red

Bulbs

Ornamental Onions (*Allium* sp.): many colors
Canna hybrids: cream, yellow, pink, red, bicolors
African Cornlily (*Ixia maculata*): red, cream + cvs.
Gladiolus: bloom time depends on when planted
  (including Acidanthera [*G. callianthus*]—
  creamy white with maroon/brown centers and
  fragrant)
Lily (*Lilium*): many colors
Arab's Eye (*Ornithogalum arabicum*): white star
  with black center, ripe apples smell
Watsonia pyramidata: pink, white, lavender + cvs.
Calla (*Zantedeschia aethiopica*): white
  (all year, but most in spring and summer)

Artichoke

Natives

Native Buckeye (*Aesculus californica*): showy
  white to pink
Western Serviceberry (*Amelanchier alnifolia*): white
Western Spicebush (*Calycanthus occidentalis*):
  spicy-sweet dusty rose
Bush Anemone (*Carpenteria californica*): showy
  white fragrant
Farewell-to-Spring/Godetia (*Clarkia amoena*):
  pink, lavender
Monkey Flower (*Diplacus aurantiacus*): yellow to
  orange (+ white, red, pink cvs.)
St. Catherine's Lace (*Erigeron giganteum*): white
  to pink
Coral Bells (*Heuchera micrantha*): white (+ rose,
  pink cvs.)
Toyon (*Heteromeles arbutifolia*): white
Western Mock Orange (*Philadelphus lewisii*):
  white with spectacular fragrance
Penstemon (*P. heterophyllus purdyi*): blue
Matilija Poppy (*Romneya coulteri*): white and fragrant
Cleveland Sage (*Salvia clevelandii*): blue; whole
  plant is wonderfully fragrant
Purple Sage (*Salvia leucophylla*): purple to violet
Blue Elderberry (*Sambucus caerulea*): white
Snowberry (*Symphoricarpos albus*): pinkish
Woolly Blue Curls (*Trichostema lanatum*): purple

Weeds

English Daisy (*Bellis perennis*): white daisy
Bull Thistle (*Cirsium vulgare*): purple heads
  (from June)
Poison Hemlock (*Conium maculatum*): big flat
  white umbels
Fennel (*Foeniculum vulgare*): yellow umbels
Pineapple Weed (*Matricaria matricarioides*):
  yellowish green, with pineapple fragrance
Sheep Sorrel/Sour Dock (*Rumex acetosella*):
  white wands
Milk Thistle (*Silybum marianum*): purple globose
  heads (from May)

FRUIT COLOR

Barberry (*Berberis* sp.): blue-black
Native Strawberry (*Fragaria chiloensis*): red
Oregon Grape (*Mahonia aquifolium*): blue-black
Native Pink-Flowering Currant (*Ribes sanguineum
  glutinosm*): blue-black (from late spring)
Native Thimbleberry (*Rubus parviflorus*): red
  (from late June)
Native Blackberry (*Rubus vitifolius*): black

Fennel

JUNE

June contains the turning point of summer, Midsummer's Day, the Summer Solstice on June 20, as delicate pink **farewell-to-spring** (*Clarkia/Godetia*) takes the place of poppies on the hillsides. (If you interplanted them with poppies, you're getting an extended show.) However, although our weather gets warmer, we rarely get summer weather in June; the famous Bay Area summer fog-sun cycle, which starts now (several days of fog clearing to a week or so of warm weather, followed again by fog), keeps us much cooler than folks further inland. Fog drip in summer in the Berkeley hills directly opposite the Golden Gate (where the trees condense it) is 10 inches—half Berkeley's total annual rainfall! Because of the fog, June days typically start out cool and gray, but by midday we can be overheated in the clothes we huddled in in the morning. This is the time for layers of clothing, so that we can strip off unneeded sweaters and jackets as the weather warms each day.

Nevertheless, hot weather-loving evergreens, such as **oleander, pyracantha,** and **agapanthus,** and deciduous plants which bloom on "new" wood (wood which has grown since the start of the spring growing season), such as **crape myrtle,** *Buddleia, Albizia,* **jacaranda, trumpetvine,** and **hybrid roses,** are putting on leaves and preparing to bloom.

With the warmer weather upon us, watering becomes necessary for non-drought-tolerant and non-Mediterranean climate plants. Strong summer afternoon winds, which start now, don't help this situation. Meanwhile, most of our natives start to return to dormancy (except the **monkey flower,** which is in full bloom now), and the annual grasses which have covered our hills since the coming of the Euro-Americans are nearly all brown. Bur clover (*Medicago polymorpha*) and foxtail (wild barley) seeds stick to socks. If you're just breaking ground for a garden now, (shame on you!), don't try to do it all in one weekend. Take it easy in the warmer weather.

PLANTING

Don't plant now if you can help it; if you must, try to give the new plant as much shade as you can from whatever shelter you can devise until it starts to get its roots out of its old root ball, or at least until it perks up and starts new growth. (Now, as always, plants planted from a container need much more water at first than they got in the container since the water in their root balls will tend to dissipate into surrounding dryer soils.) A few heat-loving plants do all right if planted now, including **gaillardia, lavender, black-eyed Susan** (*Rudbeckia hirta*), **mealy-cup sage** (*Salvia farinacea*), and **zinnias. Herbs** may also still be planted. Another exception is **leek,** which can be planted in June for October to January harvest. Also a late crop of **corn** (i.e., Silver Queen) can be sown in the garden between June 25 and July 5. If you do buy any plants, check to see if they're rootbound from being in the pot so long (roots trying to escape out the drainage hole and/or circling around the inner edge of the pot), and be sure to scarify (roughen the exterior surface of) their root ball if they are.

Calla
(Zantedeschia aethiopica)

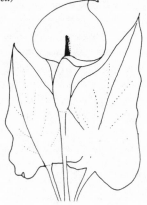

If you're going to order fall-blooming bulbs, such as **autumn "crocus"/meadow saffron** (*Colchicum autumnale*), **iris, spider lily** (*Lycoris*), **Nerine, Sternbergia,** or **Zephyranthes,** or fall- or winter-blooming annuals, now is the time to send for them.

WATERING AND MAINTENANCE

Keep watering trees and shrubs that need it. When doing any watering, be careful not to use the hot water that first comes out of the hose when you open the faucet. Stake and tie tall plants such as **dahlias, delphiniums, hollyhocks, lilies, gladiolus, corn, tomatoes**, etc. Keep composting, mulching to conserve moisture, and fertilizing (especially any annuals planted last month). Weed.

PRUNING

June is a good time to direct plant growth; shaping done now can minimize winter pruning. Also shear faded **spring-flowering annuals. Spring-flowering perennials** may bloom again if their flowers are cut back now. Cut **everlastings** (strawflowers [*Helichrysum*], statice and ammobium) to encourage growth, as well as for cut flowers. Make potpourris with flower petals. Start drying flowers for winter flower arrangements.

INSECTS AND DISEASES

About this time of year (or during the first really warm period after the rains—even in fall), **termites** start to fly in the East Bay. They look like flying ants, and they are doing their annual mating flight, looking for a new place to start a colony. If they're noticeable around your house or yard, this may be the sign of a termite infestation under the house or very nearby. Also, check your yard carefully for standing pools or puddles of water that might serve as **mosquito-**breeding grounds. If you do have a mosquito problem, remember that they are mainly active at sundown, and keeping children in for an hour or so will cut down the number of bites (and scratching) considerably. The Alameda County Mosquito Abatement District (783–7744) will also be happy to stock ponds with gambusias, a mosquito-larvae-loving little fish.

GATHERING

Late June is your first chance to go berrying in the hills. **Native blackberries** and **thimbleberries** start to fruit, and if you're lucky, you might also find the fruit of **fuchsia-flowered gooseberry.** Another fruit to look for is that of the **pink-flowering currant,** which ripens in late spring, but just might still be around. Don't pick these fruits next to roads though; they may have been sprayed with pesticide.

Shaggy parasol mushrooms (*Lepiota rhacodes*) start to appear now (until the cold of December) under Monterey cypress trees, especially those planted in sandy soil, as well as in leaf compost piles. These warm-weather-loving edibles are cinnamon brown above and white underneath, with smooth caps that break up into shaggy scales as they mature.

HARVESTING

If your **fruit trees** are dropping some of their small fruit now, this may be a healthy sign. "June-drop" of fruit is the way fruit trees make sure they haven't grown too much fruit for the amount of water and nutrients available. In fact, this is a prime time to "fruit-thin" your fruit trees if they aren't doing it themselves. This is done by giving them a good shake or two to loosen any not well-secured fruit. Fruit-thinning allows the tree to put its energy into fewer, larger, healthier fruits.

June is the main month for local **cherries,** so enjoy them now. If you planted in March/April, your cool-season crops should be ripening, even the potatoes and broccoli. (Potatoes are mature when the plants start to die down. If you planted early enough to harvest now, you still have time to plant another crop of any warm-season vegetable in their place, with four months to reach harvest.) Don't worry if your early **squash** and **zucchini** flowers seem to fade without producing fruit; many of them are male and no female flowers may yet be open to cross-pollinate them. Harvest **shallots** as they start to dry out and go dormant; **garlic** and **onions** mature with the day length, so they'll probably be ready to harvest from the end of June into mid-July.

Speaking of harvests, June is the prime time to go to the pound and get yourself a **kitten!**

JUNE EVENTS

Alstroemeria Festival—U.C. Botanical Garden, Berkeley

RECIPES

Zucchini Bread

Makes 2 loaves

5 eggs, beaten
1⅛ cup oil
2 cups sugar
1½ tsp grated lemon peel
¾ tsp orange extract
½ tsp vanilla
3 cups grated zucchini (or other summer squash)
2 cups whole wheat flour
2 cups white flour
1¼ tsp salt
¾ tsp cinnamon
½ tsp ginger
1½ tsp baking soda
3 tsp baking powder
¾ cup chopped nuts (sunflower seeds and peanuts are nice)

Beat together well eggs, oil, and sugar; then stir in the rest of the first group of ingredients. Combine second group; mix with first group; then add nuts.

Bake in 2 greased and floured 9x5-inch loaf pans at 350 degrees for 1 hour. Cool in pans until bread turns out, then cool on wire rack.

Mexican Zucchini–Avocado Salad

Serves 4 to 8

4 small zucchini (or other summer squash) (about 1 lb), cut into ¼ inch slices
8 green onions, sliced
1 Tb vegetable oil
1 medium avocado
1 Tb lemon juice
1 small green pepper, coarsely shredded or chopped
Dressing:
¼ cup vegetable oil
2 Tb vinegar
½ tsp salt
Dash of pepper

Sauté zucchini and green onions in heated oil, stirring constantly, until zucchini is crisp-tender, about 3 minutes.

Refrigerate 2 hours or more.

Cut avocado into ¼ inch slices, and sprinkle with lemon juice.

Add green pepper, prepare dressing by combining all ingredients, dress salad, and toss.

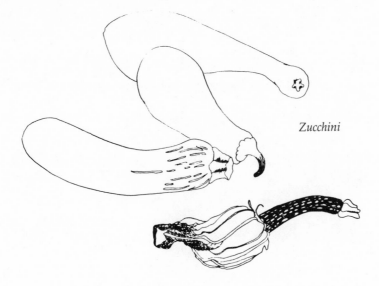

Zucchini

JULY

School has ended and vacations have started. Evenings are long, and there's plenty of time to work outside, but if you've been keeping your garden up, there's not much that needs to be done, except plenty of watering. It's not a great time to plant anything. So relax, sit on the porch, and enjoy the garden. (If you thought ahead, perhaps a grape or other deciduous vine is in leaf now and providing shade.) And start harvesting the fruits of your labors.

WATERING

This is a critical time for watering in California horticulture, so let's give the "don'ts" first because they're so important. *Don't* water any California **native perennials** (unless they are under two years old). They are adapted to our climate to such a degree that established ones develop problems if they get watered now. *Don't* water *any* **oaks.** If, unfortunately, they are planted in your lawn, you'll have to choose between the lawn and the oak. *Don't* water ground cover **junipers,** so commonly used in the Bay Area as front lawn substitutes. Watering them during the summer causes dieback, which leaves ugly brown areas, since junipers don't stump-sprout. Be careful not to overwater **citrus;** they actually produce more fruit if given a minimum of water. Also, don't overwater **tomatoes** after their fruits color. This prevents skin-slipping. Annuals and perennials that do not need too much watering include *Celosia, Coreopsis,* **hollyhock, petunia, portulaca,** *Rudbeckia,* **verbena,** *Vinca.* **Bougainvilleas** get better color if they are not watered until their soil is dry (also don't fertilize or prune them; their color comes on new growth).

Do water everything else, but especially **fuchsias, hydrangeas, cigar plant, shrimp plant,** some **ferns,** and **gardenias.** These plants are in the high point of their bloom or growth time and really using water. Annual plants that need lots of water include **ageratum, lobelia, snapdragons,** and **zinnias; dahlias** and **tuberous begonias** are among the perennials that do. Remember that deciduous plants use the same total amount of water during the year as do evergreens, but require 40 percent more water per day in the summer. Also, drought-tolerant plants *must* be regularly watered during their first few summers until they become well established.

Continue to deep-water trees and shrubs that need it, but be sure not to water right around their crown area. Don't overhead-water **tomatoes, strawberries, beans, squash,** and **melons;** these plants don't like their leaves to get wet. This helps prevent powdery mildew from getting established on the leaves, and the plants seem to grow better in general. If you can afford to invest in a drip-irrigation system, you'll find these plants do much better with it.

Keeping a good mulch cover over the surface of your garden helps reduce the amount of water plants need now. Keep fertilizing.

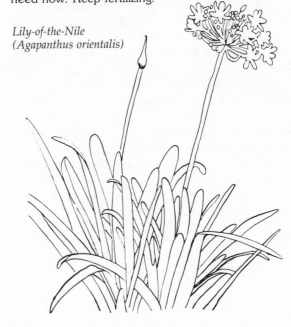

Lily-of-the-Nile
(Agapanthus orientalis)

PRUNING AND DIVIDING

July, as soon as they're finished bearing, is the time to prune the old canes off **caneberries** (**boysen, logan, olallie**) (i.e., the canes that fruited last year). If you wait to do it until the new canes start to grow, you may cut them off accidentally as well. If you're growing **chrysanthemums,** they need to be fertilized every two weeks from now until they bloom. **Dahlias** are just opening; remove blooms for display (this reduces weight and encourages more blossoms), water, and keep tied to stakes. **Irises** should be dug up, or at least have their old leaves removed, to prevent diseases from carrying over until next year. Hybrid spring-flowering bulbs which don't rebloom well in California (**tulips, hyacinths,** *Ranunculus*) can be dug up and refrigerated now, although in the East Bay they don't have to be. All bulbs which are getting crowded can be dug up and divided.

HARVESTING

Bush and pole beans, squash, and other plants you started in March should be harvestable now; if you live in a warm pocket, even some of the warm-season crops may be ready. Guatemalan **Reed avocados** should ripen between July and September. **Corn** starts to ripen July 1 (until the end of September), and **plums** from July 1 through August. **Peaches** arrive in the stores early July through early September. In late July and in August, it's picking time for most **grapes. Gravenstein apple** season is late July through early August. If you'd like to pick them yourself from the commercial farms of Napa and Sonoma, contact Napa County Farming Trails (4075 Solano Avenue, Napa, CA 94558); Sonoma County Farm Trails (P.O. Box 6674, Santa Rosa, CA 95406) for the locations of farms with U-Pick operations. Harvest Time in Brentwood (P.O. Box O, Brentwood, CA 94513) lists farms in eastern Contra Costa County.

Check your garden to see if you have any edible flowers like **nasturtiums, bee balm/bergamot** (*Monarda*), **borage,** or **daylilies,** which can be put into salads. If you have a **pyracantha, crabapple,** or **apricot** that is not fruiting, remember that these may fruit only in alternate years. **Carob** trees also have a sparse harvest in alternate years.

JULY EVENTS

Tuberous Begonia Show—Golden Gate Park Conservatory

San Francisco Branch American Fuchsia Society Show—Golden Gate Park Hall of Flowers

San Leandro Fuchsia Society—Macy's Bayfair Store

Peach Harvest Festival—Smyrna Park at Fowler and Moffett Streets, Ceres (near Modesto)

Cantaloupe Roundup—Firebaugh Park on Q Street, Firebaugh (west of Fresno)

Pear Fair—Bates School, Courtland (south of Sacramento)

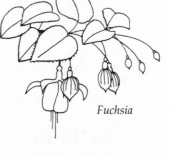

Fuchsia

RECIPES

Portofino Tuna Soup

Serves 2 to 4

A great, easy-to-make summer recipe for your pole or bush bean harvest. You may want to wait to cook it with your green peppers and tomatoes when they can be harvested.

6½ or 7 oz can tuna in oil
1 small onion, cut bite-size
1 medium green pepper, cut bite-size
1 or more cloves garlic, minced or pressed
2 cups chicken broth
6 fresh tomatoes, cut bite-size
½ lb fresh green beans
½ tsp salt
¼ tsp dried oregano leaves, crumbled
¼ tsp hot pepper sauce or dash of cayenne
½ cup fresh parsley, chopped

Drain the oil from the can of tuna into a large saucepan. Add the onion, green pepper, and garlic. Sauté until the onion is tender but not brown.

Stir in the tuna and the rest of the ingredients. Bring to a boil, and simmer 10 minutes. Serve with crusty French bread.

African Bean Salad and Senegalese Curry Soup

Serves 4

Black-eyed peas are a crop not grown by too many Bay Area gardeners, and it is not certain how they would do here. If you've never tasted them any other way but dried and rehydrated, you may wonder why anyone is interested in growing them at all. But a fresh black-eyed pea is a gourmet delight and can now be found in some of the East Bay's fresh produce markets. This is a good time of year to look for them, and once you've developed a taste for them and tried planting them along with other beans, this would be the time to enjoy them fresh off the vine.

African Bean Salad

2 cups (10 oz) fresh black-eyed peas (other peas optional)
2 onions, diced
2 or more cloves garlic, diced or mashed
2 Tb oil
4 Tb or less tomato paste (freeze the rest of the can for later use)
12 oz cooked cleaned shrimp, coarsely chopped if large
2 lb ham, diced
2 Tb lemon juice

Cook the peas in water to cover for 45 minutes. If much excess water is left, drain.

Sauté the onion and garlic in oil until soft. Stir in tomato paste, shrimp, and ham. Remove from heat, and stir in peas.

Salt to taste, and sprinkle with lemon juice. Can be served cold.

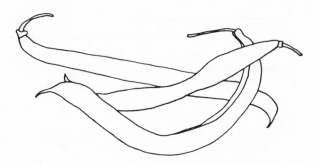

Pole or Green Beans

Senegalese Curry Soup

3 Tb butter
1 onion, minced
1 small green apple, chopped
1½–2 tsp curry powder
1½ Tb flour
3 cups chicken broth (or 15 oz can + 1 cup water)
paprika, ground coriander, salt and pepper to taste
1 egg, beaten
½ cup milk or cream or buttermilk
½ cup slivers of cooked or uncooked chicken (optional)
4 Tb chutney (optional)
chopped chives or cilantro (optional)

Melt butter; add onion, apple, curry powder, flour, and spices; then gradually blend in broth. Bring to a boil, reduce to simmer, and stir in egg and milk. Stir until thickened slightly, but do not boil.

Add chicken and chutney. If chicken is uncooked, simmer until done. Otherwise, simmer until warmed. Garnish with chives or cilantro if desired.

*Borage
(Borago officinalis)*

PLANTS WHICH START TO BLOOM IN JULY AND AUGUST

Trees

Silk Tree (*Albizia julibrissin*): spectacular pink
Goldenrain Tree (*Koelreuteria paniculata*): yellow
Crape Myrtle (*Lagerstroemia indica*): pink to red, lavender or white
Flaxleaf Paperbark (*Meleleuca linarifolia*): white, snowy
Little Leaf Linden (*Tilia cordata*): yellow and fragrant

Shrubs

Lemon Verbena (*Aloysia triphylla*): white and fragrant
Bouvardia longiflora 'Albatross': showy white and fragrant
Angel's Trumpet (*Brugmansia suaveolens*): enormous fragrant white trumpets (once called Datura)
Escallonia sp.: white to pink to red

Fuchsia sp.: many colors
Boxleaf Hebe (*Hebe odora*): white
Hydrangea sp.: many colors
Shrub Hypericum (*Hypericum beanii*): yellow
Shrimp Plant (*Justicia brandegeana*): white, but
  hidden inside coppery bronze or chartreuse bracts
Japanese Privet (*Ligustrum japonicum*): white
Turk's Cap/Wax Mallow (*Malvaviscus arboreus*):
  scarlet
Myrtle (*Myrtus communis*): white
English Laurel (*Prunus laurocerasus*): white
"Hybrid" Roses (*Rosa* sp.): many colors
Potato Vine (*Solanum jasminoides*): white
(Also other common members of the *Solanaceae*
  family including Tomato, Eggplant,
  Peppers, and Nightshade)

Ground Covers

Bear's Breach (*Acanthus mollis*): white
Lily-of-the-Nile (*Agapanthus orientalis*): blue-violet
Chamomile (*Chaemaemelum nobile*): yellow
Ground Morning Glory (*Convolvulus sabatius*):
  lavender blue
Maiden's Wreath (*Francoa ramosa*): white
Creeping St. Johnswort (*Hypericum calycinum*):
  yellow
Lantana camara: yellow, orange, or red
Lavenders (*Lavendula dentata, L. angustifolia*):
  lavender
Mazus reptans: violet
Moss Pink (*Phlox subulata*): rose to lavender
Spring Cinquefoil (*Potentilla tabernaemontanii*):
  yellow
Pratia (*Pratia angulata*): white
Irish and Scotch Moss (*Sagina subulata*): white
Lavender Cotton (*Santolina chamaecyparissus*):
  yellow
Strawberry Geranium (*Saxifraga stolonifera*): white
Australian Bluebell Creeper (*Sollya heterophylla*):
  light blue
Woolly Lamb's Ears (*Stachys byzantina*): purple
Prostrate Germander (*Teucrium chamaedrys*
  'Prostratum'): rose to pink

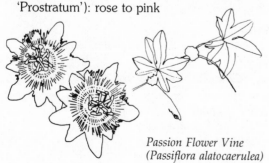

Passion Flower Vine
(*Passiflora alatocaerulea*)

Vines

Kiwi (*Actinidia chinensis*): white
Bougainvillea (*B. spectabilis*): purple (+ red cvs.)
Giant Burmese Honeysuckle (*Lonicera
  hildebrandiana*): yellow and fragrant
Bower Vine (*Pandorea jasminoides*): white
Passion Vine (*Passiflora alatocaerulea*): pink + white

Herbaceous Perennials

Love-Lies-Bleeding (*Amaranthus caudatus*): red
Feverfew (*Chrysanthemum parthenium*): white
  (+ yellow cvs.)
Dahlia: many colors (often grown as an annual
  due to frost tenderness)
Daylilies (*Hemerocallis* sp.): many colors
Snakeroot/Gayfeather (*Liatris spicata*): purple
Summer Phlox (*Phlox paniculata*): many colors
Black-Eyed Susan/Gloriosa Daisy (*Rudbeckia
  hirta*): big daisylike flowers in oranges, yellows,
  russets, mahoganys, with dark centers
Goldenrod (*Solidago* sp.): yellow plume

Annuals

Mexican Tulip Poppy (*Hunnemannia fumariifolia*):
  golden (looks very much like California Poppy)
Four o'Clock (*Mirabilis jalapa*): red to yellow to white
Marigold (*Tagetes erecta*): yellows, oranges, white
Zinnia (*Z. elegans*): many colors

Bulbs

Tuberous Begonia (*Begonia tuberosa*): many colors
Naked Lady (*Amaryllis belladonna*): big pink
  trumpet on bare stem (foliage follows with
  first rains)
Cyclamen hederifolium: many colors
Mexican Shell Flower (*Tigridia pavonia*): orange,
  pink, red, yellow, or white, with darker spotting
  on central smaller petals
Tuberose (*Polianthes tuberosa*): spikes of tubular
  fragrant white

Natives

Sagebrush (*Artemisia* sp.): yellow
Native Buckeye (*Aesculus californica*): loses its leaves
Native Fuchsia-Flowered Gooseberry (*Ribes
  speciosum*): red-purple fruits
Invader/'Himalaya' Blackberry (*Rubus procerus*):
  black fruits

Weeds

Milkweed (*Asclepias syriaca*): dull purple to pink,
  pollinated by the monarch butterfly
Bush or Mound "Morning Glory" (*Convolvulus* sp.):
  white to pink to lavender
Nightshade (*Solanum* sp.): white or purple

AUGUST

August 7 is the official calendar start of fall. **Bougainvillea, hibiscus, princess flower, verbena, lantana,** and other tropical plants come into full bloom. This is the month for **dahlias,** and Lakeside Park Gardens will be having their show. It's a wonderful time to sit outside in the garden in the warm evening air and to listen to music, eat a late snack, or just look at the moon. In fact, the Chinese and Japanese have their "Moon-Viewing festivals this month (or occasionally in September), for this is the time when the full moon seems to appear largest. Lakeside Park is usually the host of a Moon-Viewing event.

WATERING

Continue watering (see *July Watering* suggestions, p. 55). Remember that dormant **cool-season lawns** still need water. (If you've had it with lawns, this is also a prime time to dig them up, before they go to seed, and to replant them with drought-tolerant ground covers.) Keep deep-watering and lightly fertilize hybrid **roses.**

PLANTING

In August, you can again start seedlings of many **cool-season** and **perennial vegetables,** such as artichokes, cabbage, cauliflower, celery, garlic, spinach, and turnips, to be planted out in September. Plant **fall-blooming bulbs.** You can also start ordering **cool-season vegetable** seeds for your fall garden. If you're going to mail-order **bulbs for next spring's bloom,** now is the time to get out your catalogs for that too.

July through August is also a prime time for budding another type of apple onto your apple tree.

MAINTENANCE

Summer-blooming perennials (i.e., **coreopsis, delphinium,** *Nepeta,* **penstemon, Shasta daisies, yarrow, dahlias**) can be cut back for a second fall bloom. Keep fertilizing **summer-flowering annuals, container plants,** and **begonias; fuchsias** also need continued fertilization, as well as removal of fruit and faded flowers, which will keep them blooming longer; the fruit can be put up as jam.

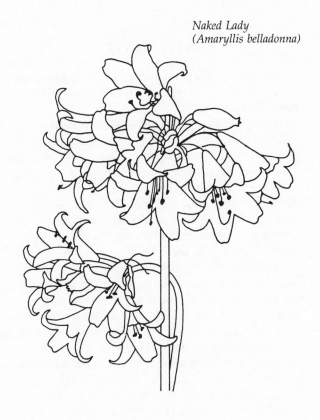

Naked Lady
(Amaryllis belladonna)

DISEASES

The warm season is a prime time for diseases in the East Bay. In particular, **powdery mildew** (which appears as a white chalky film) starts to become active now (see list of susceptible plants, p. 18). One way to discourage it is to avoid overhead watering, especially in the afternoon, as this fungus likes wet, hot conditions; replanting the plant to a sunnier, less shady location may also help. Start watching **tomato, eggplant, peppers, strawberry, potatoes,** and other susceptible plants for signs of **verticillium wilt**: not fruiting or fruit not ripening fully. (See *September Watering,* p. 65, for care, and *March Planting,* p. 36, for prevention.) Clean under fruit trees, picking up fruit mummies (dry, shriveled fruit, which can carry brown rot over to the next growing season if left lying on the ground), as well as around **azaleas, camellias,** and **rhododendrons.**

If you have an old, uncared-for fruit tree that you'd like to stimulate to new growth, try pruning it after it's finished fruiting. Summer pruning, though unorthodox, can help rejuvenate older fruit trees.

GATHERING

Late summer is another good time to go **berrying** in the East Bay hills; **elderberries** and **huckleberries** should be ripe.

Bright yellow orange **sulphur shelf mushrooms** (*Laetiporus sulphureus*) appear on eucalyptus trees during August and September. Called "Chicken of the Woods," they are flat, wavy, shelflike, overlapping half-circles growing out of stumps or, occasionally, out of a wound in a live tree. They have a meaty taste, and the tender edges are said to be quite a treat; however, never eat them raw, and be careful when tasting them for the first time.

If you've been tilling ground to put in a new planting, you may be lucky enough to find those prizes of the mushroom world, **morels,** poking up out of the moist soil. They are using the sugars from roots that have been cut off in the process of tilling. Although more commonly found in other parts of the world in the spring, they can appear—most unpredictably—at any time of year in California. If you think you've got them, try calling someone from the San Francisco Mycological Society to verify this rare treat.

HARVESTING

It's time to get out and harvest! Especially important to keep checking (daily!) are the **zucchini** and other **squash.** The fruit from these can easily be hidden under foliage and get big and pithy almost overnight. Also, keep picking **beans** off their vines to keep them from producing mealy, dry fruit.

In August, **tomatoes** may start to be pickable (until the end of October or so). By mid-August, **prunes** ripen. In late August, **Jonathan** and **Delicious apples** are ready to eat, and **summer pears,** such as **Bartlett,** should also be ready to pick about now (pick them before they're fully ripe or they'll get mealy). Mexican **Mexicola avocados** ripen August to October. **Sapote** fruit is ready to eat from now until November.

AUGUST EVENTS

San Francisco County Fair—Golden Gate Park Hall of Flowers

Dahlia Show—Lakeside Park, Oakland

San Leandro Dahlia Show—Bancroft Junior High School

Sixteen Flower Societies Show—Golden Gate Park Hall of Flowers

Moon-Viewing Celebration—Lakeside Park, Oakland

Garlic Festival—Gilroy (Hwy. 101, Santa Cruz County)

Gravenstein Apple Fair—Ragle Park, Sebastopol (near Santa Rosa)

Zucchini Festival—Kennedy Park, Hayward

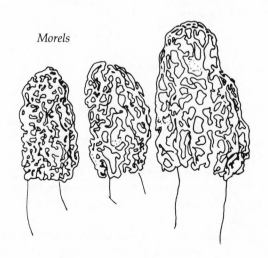

Morels

RECIPES

Gazpacho Soup with Zucchini Frittata and Fresh Corn

Serves 4 to 6

Spanish Gazpacho Soup

4 cups chicken broth
4 medium tomatoes, chopped
2 Tb olive oil
6 to 8 Tb lime juice (about 3 limes)
1 small red onion, diced
1 or 2 green or red bell peppers, chopped
1 or 2 stalks celery, chopped

Mix all ingredients together, blend in blender if smoothness is desired, chill as long as possible, and serve.

Optional additions: avocado, cucumber, oregano, wine, vinegar, garlic, cumin, watercress.

Zucchini Frittata

1½ lb young zucchini (about 4½ cups chopped), chopped finely
1 medium onion, (diced)
3 Tb olive oil
6 eggs
basil, minced, to taste
salt and pepper to taste

Sauté onions and zucchini in olive oil in a large skillet until soft.

Beat eggs with basil, salt, and pepper.

Spread the vegetables evenly around the pan, and pour the beaten eggs over them. Cook at low heat until the eggs set.

Turn over by flipping onto a plate, then sliding it from the plate back into the skillet. Cook briefly until firm all the way through.

Fresh Sweet Corn

Boil a pot of water big enough to fit all the corn you want to eat in it. Then, 10 minutes before you're ready to eat, go out to the backyard and pick the corn, shuck it, *run* back into the house, and pop it into the pot for 3 to 5 minutes.

Bengali Stewed Vegetables with Plantains

Serves 4

3 Tb vegetable oil
2 tsp cumin seeds
1 large potato
1 unripe (green) plantain
1 small eggplant, unpeeled
3 large outer leaves of cabbage
1 zucchini
1 tsp ground turmeric
1 tsp ground cumin
½ tsp ground pepper
¾ tsp salt
1 tomato, chopped
lemon wedges (optional)

Cut all vegetables to bite-size cubes or slices. Heat oil in a large frying pan, and fry cumin seeds until they become aromatic and darken. Add vegetables successively in the order given, stirring to coat them with oil.

After the zucchini has been added, add the spices, plus 1½ cups water, and mix well. Cover and cook 10 minutes.

Finally, add tomato, cover, and cook until vegetables are tender but not mushy, about 5 to 10 minutes more.

Serve with rice and lemon wedges.

Sweet Corn

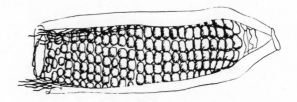

SEPTEMBER

There's a lot of confusion about when "fall" or "autumn" is in the East Bay, and rightly so, because this traditional autumn month (the Autumn Equinox is September 23) is paradoxically the start of the East Bay's "summer." The fogs subside, and in between the early rains we have our warmest weather of the year and our only dependable beach weather (the San Francisco Bay's water is at its warmest, too). For the hills, this is our "yellow" season; wildflowers have all gone brown (except for *Zauschneria,* called "California fuchsia," which is in brilliant red bloom). Red **poison oak** leaves are almost the only bright color in the hills. But in the gardens, **bougainvillea, hibiscus, princess flower,** and **lantana** are providing color. On an evening walk, you can sometimes catch a whiff of the **night-blooming jasmine,** of *Sarcococca,* the shade plant, or of **osmanthus** During a hot summer, this is the month to visit a cool Japanese garden: perhaps the one just outside Strybing Botanical Gardens in San Francisco, Hakone in Saratoga, or the smaller one in Lakeside Park in Oakland. But there's plenty to do in the garden this month, as the first rains start the greening process again. September is an important pivotal month in the East Bay.

PLANTING

To the surprise of most newcomers, September and October are prime months to plant in the East Bay (as well as most of California). All landscape trees, shrubs, ground covers, grasses, and many annuals can be planted now, before the rains start. The soil is still warm from summer, encouraging strong root growth, but leaf and top growth slows with the lowering temperatures, reducing water loss.

How it's done is crucial to your soil's future health. In order to break up the ground for planting, wet it thoroughly, then WAIT two to five days (two days if the weather's really hot, up to five days if it's cool). You're waiting until the ground is "friable," has "tilth," is "workable," that is, all those ways to say that the soil is at the right point on the scale between wet and dry so that a shovel goes in easily but the soil does not stick to it.

These months are a perfect time for **neighborhood tree plantings,** with plenty of potluck refreshments to help celebrate the occasion. Remember, though, rain in this period is unpredictable, and your new seedlings will need plenty of watering until the rains start for real. Then they will have a whole season of luxurious rainfall before they have to face our dry summers. (Note: Drought-tolerant plants also need a summer or two of regular watering before they are able to fend for themselves.)

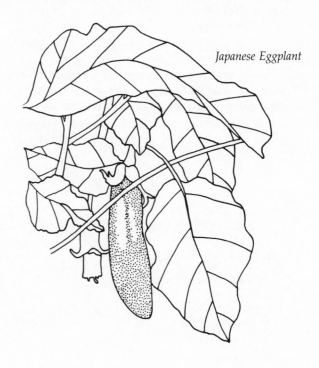

Japanese Eggplant

63

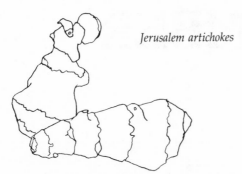

Jerusalem artichokes

September is also a good time to sow **cool-season lawns,** fertilize them, put down sod, and reseed bare spots. Dormant cool-season lawns (bentgrass, bluegrass, fescue, rye) should start to stir mid-September.

September is the time to plant **"winter annuals"** (the spring flowerers listed in the Bloom Lists for November through February). **Spring-blooming bulbs** also start being shipped in late September through October. If you're going to buy them at the nursery, do it by early October, while there is a good selection. Store them (especially **tulips** and **hyacinths**) in a refrigerator for four to six weeks (to plant in cooler October). **Tip-cuttings** can still be propagated.

September is the only time of year that **saffron crocus** (*Crocus sativus*) bulbs can be purchased for planting. Although well adapted to our dry summers and wet winters, they will need much irrigating in September (unless we're having an unusually rainy month) to produce their gorgeous blue-violet flowers, each with its edible orange and red stigma.

Recent studies have shown that **California poppies, lupines, clarkias, blue-eyed grass,** and other native wildflower seeds can best be sown this month (even though most package directions instruct you to wait until just before the winter rains start).

Radicchio

VEGETABLE PLANTING

For vegetable gardeners, this is also a prime planting time. Best planted now are the cool-weather lovers: the **leafy vegetables** and the **root vegetables.** Included among the leafy vegetables to plant now are almost all the common vegetables of the *Brassica* (cabbage) family: **broccoli** and **cauliflower** (actually we eat the flowers of these two), **Brussels sprouts, all cabbages** (including **bok choy**), **collards, kale, mustards,** and **broccoli raab**; also **lettuces, celery, chicory, Swiss chard, endives, spinach, garden cress** (*Lepidium sativum*—not the same as watercress), **chickweed, corn salad/lamb's lettuce/mache, roquette/rocket/arugula, lambsquarter, purslane,** and **miner's lettuce/claytonia.**

Root vegetables to plant now include **burdock/gobo** (careful—can be invasive!), **carrots, parsnips, salsify** and **scorzonera/black salsify, kohlrabi, potatoes, Jerusalem artichokes, beets,** and two more of the cabbage family (cole) crops: **radishes, rutabagas** and **turnips** (which are also grown for their greens).

Although **potatoes** are traditionally planted in the spring, they can also be planted now in the East Bay; the tops will be killed by frost, but the tubers will be very tasty. (I've had some trouble finding a catalog source that will mail potato seed-eyes at this time. Evidently mail-order companies don't believe that potatoes can be started now, or they just don't have any ready to sell. You may have to replant by saving your own seed-eyes. Store-bought potatoes may be usable, although some are sprayed with hormones to keep them from sprouting.) **Carrots,** another traditional spring crop, can also be grown during the winter in the East Bay. Get them off to a good start now, while the weather is still warm, and they will get through the winter fine and be harvestable for early spring eating.

Also plantable now are perennials such as **rhubarb, artichoke, chayote, lemon balm** (*Melissa officinalis*), **sorrel, salad burnet, winter savory, currants, Florence fennel,** and **gooseberries**; "weeds" like **dock, nettles, sow thistle, dandelions,** and **shepherd's purse; fava ("broad") beans** (as a food crop or to enrich the soil as a ground cover), although some sources consider October to December to be a better seeding time for these, and **snap peas**; and members of the Allium genus, including **garlic** and **shallots** (neither of which will be ready until summer but which need a long growing season), **"bulbing" onions, green onions** (also called bunching onions or scallions; includes Welsh onions), **rocambole,** and **leeks.**

It's a good idea to stagger your seedlings of these so that they don't all mature at once. Try starting some each week.

If your garden is already started, now is the time to start interplanting these winter crops. If you are just starting a garden, be sure *not* to leave your soil-breaking until the heavy rains start in late October. Also, getting your crops in as early as possible will give them time to get established before the cold weather starts.

Bottlebrush (Callistemon and Meleleuca sp.)

FERTILIZING

Of course, you'll want to fertilize cool-season crops that you plant this month. Fall is a growing season for many plants in the East Bay, so this is also a good time to fertilize plants that you want to help along. Keep fertilizing late summer bloomers (although this should be your last fertilization of citrus or other subtropical plants). Start checking acid-soil-loving plants like **azaleas, camellias, rhododendrons, hydrangeas, fuchsias, primulas, pieris,** and **ericas** to see if they are showing signs of iron chlorosis (yellowing of new leaves, with green veins between yellow areas); this may be more noticeable as the weather turns colder. Dig "hot" fertilizers (rabbit and chicken manure, bloodmeal) and/or compost into vegetable garden soil so it can get worked in by the rains. You can help your fruit trees (including citrus) by starting a monthly application of high phosphorus and high potassium fertilizer (no nitrogen!) from now until April 1. (If you do, it's good to balance the acidity this creates by applying lime once a year.) Apply the fertilizer evenly from about 2 feet from the trunk to the "drip line" (directly below the ends of the branches); rain will carry it down to the roots.

WATERING

You'll want to water more heavily during the hot spells this month and next, although the early rains will help. Keep following the suggestions for dry-season watering noted for July and August. Leaf edges of susceptible plants will tend to blacken now if there is too much boron (salts) in the soil. Watch carefully for signs of verticillium wilt in **tomatoes, eggplants, peppers, potatoes, strawberries,** etc. You can help the plant to fight off the effect of the fungus if you keep it well watered. (But be sure not to overwater these plants if they have no problem with verticillium wilt; otherwise, you may cause the skins of their fruits to split.)

PRUNING AND DIVIDING

Don't prune anything now if possible. There are numerous pathogens active during our warm season in the East Bay, and the pruning cuts you make will allow easy access. Wait a bit more until the weather cools and they really have started to go dormant before pruning deciduous fruit trees.

Do remove any remaining fruit mummies and fallen leaves around fruit trees. Rake the ground clean of these and all other fallen plant parts. This is also a good time to start removing dead flowers from summer flowerers to keep them looking fresh and promote flowering next season. **Marguerites** should be cut back a third to a half (without cutting into their woody part, however). **Tuberous begonias** should be dead-headed, but leave their stalks until they break off by themselves, and continue watering and light fertilization.

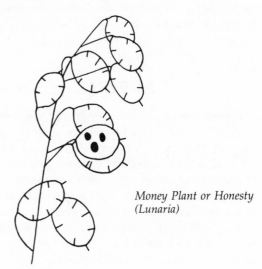

Money Plant or Honesty (Lunaria)

Nut Sedge
(Cyperus esculentus)

Camellias should have all the fat flower buds at their branch tips removed except one or two and most other buds removed to leave buds at least 4 inches apart. **Chrysanthemums** should be watered daily on hot days, tied to stakes, thinned to one bud at each stem tip.

WEEDING

September is a good time to weed and take out overgrowth before the plants you don't want set seed and start to grow again in our wet winter season. The time you take to do this now will save you more work in the spring. September and October are also good months to remove any woody plants that you might be able to use for firewood and store them in a dry place before the rains start.

SPECIAL

Poinsettias, which left to their own rhythms "bloom"—their bracts redden—in January, can be made to bloom early if they receive 13 hours of complete, absolutely unbroken darkness per day for 3 months. Cover them with a dark cloth or put them in a completely darkened room, and don't allow them to be exposed to light for even one second during this dark period. In order to be ready for Christmas, you've got start by at least September 25. It's not hard to do if you keep to the schedule.

If your **naked lady** (*Amaryllis belladonna*) or **spider lily** (*Lycoris*) needs to be transplanted, now is the time to do it, before they start to put on new foliage. **Oriental poppies** (*Papaver orientale*) can be divided now before they start their fall growth.

GATHERING

September is a major gathering month. Now is the time to collect seeds for next season (remember that some of your garden plants are hybrids and will not produce exactly the same characteristics by seed). Check parks near you for these, as well as your yard. Ask neighbors for seeds from plants you like. Gather nuts, flowers for dried winter arrangements, and petals for potpourris.

HARVESTING

Finally, the East Bay gets enough heat to catch up with warmer regions; the fruits of **tomatoes, corn, cucumbers, eggplants, peppers, beans,** and **squash** should all be ripening. **Grapes** and some **pears** fruit in the Bay Area September through October. Mid-September to early November is a second season for **figs,** this time growing on "new" wood. At the end of the month, there is also a second **raspberry** season lasting to mid-November, and **Rome apples** start to ripen (also to mid-November). Don't pick your **kiwis**; they're not fully ready.

What to do with all that bounty? This is a good time for drying some of your harvest for later use. Or trade some of your extra zucchini for someone else's extra tomatoes.

SEPTEMBER EVENTS

American Fuchsia Society—Golden Gate Park Hall of Flowers

Dahlia Society of California Show—Golden Gate Park Hall of Flowers

Raisin Festival—Kerckhoff Park at Madera and G Streets, Kerman (just west of Fresno)

Artichoke Festival—Castroville (between Santa Cruz and Monterey)

Mendocino Apple Show—Boonville Fairgrounds (southwest of Ukiah)

Raisin Festival—El Monte Park, Dinuba (southeast of Fresno)

Plant Sale—U.C. Botanical Garden

Grape Harvest—Napa, Sonoma, Amador Valley, etc.

RECIPES

Gado Gado

An Indonesian Hot-Day Vegetable Salad
Serves 6 to 8

4 or 5 carrots, cut into long strips
½ lb green beans, cut into 2-inch diagonal lengths
½ head cabbage, thinly sliced
½ lb bean sprouts
2 hard-boiled eggs, quartered or sliced
2 tomatoes, quartered or sliced
1 cucumber, sliced

Blanch the carrots for a few minutes, add the beans and cabbage, then add the sprouts, and steam for 1 more minute. Drain and chill.

Arrange on individual plates, and top with the other ingredients.

Serve with **Peanut Sauce Dressing:**

½ cup hot water or chicken broth
½ cup peanut butter or sesame seed paste (tahini)
1 clove garlic, pressed
2 Tb brown sugar
2 Tb vinegar or lemon juice
¼ to ½ tsp crushed dried chilies
½ tsp salt

Gradually add water to peanut butter, stirring until smooth. Blend in other ingredients.

Also good over blanched zucchini or other squash.

The Chinese of Hunan make a summer salad with very similar ingredients. They add to the above: soy sauce, white wine, sesame oil, minced fresh ginger, hot mustard, scallions, and cilantro. Slivers of chicken may also be added, as well as bean threads or rice noodles.

Squash Soup with Lemon and Basil

Serves 4

Yet another delicious way to use your abundant supply of zucchini and squash!

2 Tb olive oil
1 large sweet red or white onion, diced
3 or more garlic cloves, diced or mashed
4 cups chicken broth
1 medium carrot
3 medium zucchini
3 medium summer squash
3 Tb fresh basil, coarsely shredded
slice of rind from ½–1 lemon

Heat the oil in a large saucepan. Sauté the onion and garlic for five minutes, until transparent. Slice the carrot, zucchini, and summer squash thinly and add to the pot with the broth, basil, and lemon rind. Cook five to ten minutes more. Season with salt and pepper if desired. When the vegetables are tender enough, you may want to mash some or all of them with a potato masher to thicken the broth.

Tomato

PLANTS WHICH START TO BLOOM IN SEPTEMBER AND OCTOBER

Trees
New Zealand Lacebark (*Hoheria populnea*): white

Shrubs
Trinidad Flame Bush (*Calliandra tweedii*):
  red bottlebrush
Lemon Bottlebrush (*Callistemon citrinus*):
  red bottlebrush (second bloom time)
Japanese Aralia (*Fatsia japonica*): white, closely
  followed by clusters of black fruits
Pink Meleleuca (*Meleleuca nesophila*): pink
  bottlebrush
Princess Flower/Pleroma (*Tibouchina urvilleana*):
  showy violet (blooms all year, but especially
  during hot weather)

Shrubs with blooms that are nearly invisible, but very fragrant
Night-Blooming Jasmine (*Cestrum nocturnum*)
Holly-Leaf Osmanthus (*Osmanthus heterophyllus*)
Sarcococca sp.

Ground Covers
Dwarf Plumbago (*Ceratostigma plumbaginoides*):
  gentian blue
Weeping Lantana (*Lantana montevidensis*):
  lavender-magenta
Big Blue Lily Turf (*Liriope muscari*): purple
Prostrate Myoporum (*Myoporum parvifolium*): white
Creeping Mint (*Mentha requienii*): pink to violet
Plumbago (*Plumbago auriculata*): blue
Mexican Bush Sage (*Salvia leucantha*): violet

Vines
Common Trumpet Creeper (*Campsis radicans*):
  orange to red
Silver Lace Vine (*Polygonum aubertii*): white
Cape Honeysuckle (*Tecomaria capensis*): orange
  to red (+ yellow cvs.)
Black-Eyed Susan Vine (*Thunbergia alata*):
  yellow with black centers

Herbaceous Perennials
Marguerite (*Chrysanthemum frutescens*): white,
  yellow, pink (second bloom time)
Chrysanthemum (*C. morifolium*): many colors
  (usually grown as an annual)

Bulbs
Zephyranthes sp.: white, yellow, or rose-pink
  (blooms after the rains)

Natives
California Fuchsia (*Zauschneria californica*):
  red fuchsialike

FALL FRUIT COLOR (not edible or not very tasty)
Hawthorn (*Craetaegus* sp.): red (tree)
Cotoneaster sp.: red (shrub)
Native Salal (*Gaultheria shallon*): black
  (ground cover)
Native Toyon (*Heteromeles arbutifolia*):
  red-orange (tree)
Holly (*Ilex aquifolium*): red (shrub)
Chinese Pistache (*Pistacia chinensis*): red (tree)
Pyracantha sp.: red (shrub)
California or Chilean Pepper (*Schinus molle*): red
  (tree)
Brazilian Pepper (*Schinus terebinthifolius*): red (tree)
Native Snowberry (*Symphoricarpos albus*): white
  (shrub)
Australian Brush Cherry (*Syzygium paniculatum*):
  purple (tree, shrub, or vine)

FALL FRUIT COLOR (edible)
Kiwi (*Actinidia chinensis*): fuzzy brown (vine)
Western Serviceberry (*Amelanchier alnifolia*):
  blue to purple (shrub)
Native Madrone (*Arbutus menziesii*): brilliant red
  or orange (tree)
Strawberry Tree (*Arbutus unedo*): rosy red
Native Manzanita (*Arctostaphylos* sp.): red-brown
  (shrub)
Native Bearberry/Kinnikinnick (*Arctostaphylos
  uva-ursi*): bright red (shrub or ground cover)
Natal Plum (*Carissa grandiflora*): red to
  purple-black (shrub)
Western Hazelnut (*Corylus cornuta*): brown
  (shrub or tree)
Persimmon (*Diospyros kaki*): orange (tree)
Olive (*Olea europaea*): black (tree)
Pomegranate (*Punica granatum*): red (shrub or tree)
  (at the same time as orange flowers)
Native Blue Elderberry (*Sambucus caerulea*):
  blue-black (Warning: *S. calicarpa racemosa*,
  a variety of Red Elderberry, is poisonous.)
Native Huckleberry (*Vaccinium ovatum*): dark blue

Weeds
Sheep Sorrel/Sour Dock (*Rumex acetosella*):
  wands have turned red
Nut Sedge (*Cyperus esculentus*): seeds turning
  red-brown

OCTOBER

October brings our first big storms, sometimes with lightning and thunder (signs of an impending storm are a change in wind direction, combined with low cloudiness). You can still plan events without worrying about rain and the weather is still warm, although starting to turn a bit cooler. Nevertheless, it's autumn everywhere else, and birds can be seen flying south, while the monarch butterflies gather in Pacific Grove and Big Sur for the winter. Ladybugs meet in their hill retreats for a breeding bonanza. Poison oak starts to drop its bright red leaves. You can start to see East Bay autumn color as **London plane trees, liquidambars, ashes,** and **maples** start to lose their leaves. The **pyracanthas** and **cotoneasters,** the seeds of which the birds have distributed everywhere around the East Bay, are covered with red berries, as are the **California peppers,** the **Chinese pistache,** and the **strawberry tree. Wisteria** and **broom** seeds can be heard popping from their pods. It's a time for wine making, chrysanthemums, olive curing, chestnut roasting, pumpkin carving, and not forgetting to turn the clock back.

PLANTING

October is California's "second spring," when cooling air, still-warm soil, and the early rains give many plants a second growth spurt. It is an excellent month for planting just about everything: trees, shrubs, natives, perennials. It's the time to plant **azaleas** and another good time for planting **strawberries.** Annuals for winter, spring, and summer bloom should be sown or their seedlings set out. Sow wildflower seeds if you haven't yet.

Cool-season lawns (bentgrass, bluegrass, fescue, rye) are growing and can still be reseeded or planted. If they are already in place, they should be returning now; thatch, aerate, and fertilize. Above all, it's time to take the **spring-blooming bulbs** out of the refrigerator and plant them as the weather turns cool. You can overplant them with annuals to mark their location.

The only things that shouldn't be planted now are deciduous shrubs and trees (they're cheaper bare-root in December) and tropical heat-lovers like citrus and bougainvillea (see *April Planting,* p. 41, for longer list), and any warm-season crops.

Keep stagger-planting **cool-season vegetables,** and keep collecting seeds. **Onion sets** can be planted from October until April. If you're not going to plant an area after you've harvested your summer vegetables, sow a cover crop to keep the soil in place and enrich it. **Asparagus** for planting bare-root should be ordered in October.

When planting, a very important rule to keep in mind is *don't work the soil when it's soggy!* Digging soggy soil is the best way to break down the soil structure which is the best thing our clay soils have going for them. It will lead to poorer air and water retention and poorer plant growth. Wait a few days for a dry spell (see note on tilth under *September Planting,* p. 63).

If you didn't get a chance in September, this is still a good time to prepare the soil for spring planting by adding "hot" fertilizers.

October is also the time for cutting scions of trees you want to graft. Store them in the refrigerator until spring.

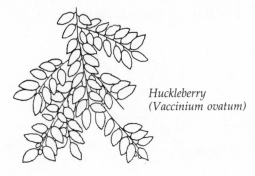

*Huckleberry
(Vaccinium ovatum)*

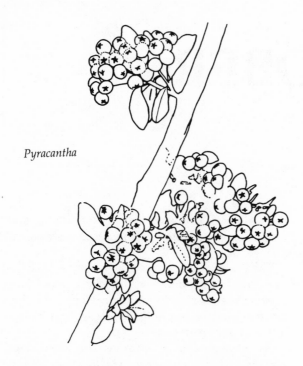

Pyracantha

FERTILIZING AND WATERING

Watering can be slowed when occasional rains do more of the job. Most plants should *not* be fertilized now as they are starting to slow their growth for winter. However, *do* fertilize September-planted trees, shrubs, and ground covers (a month after they were planted), then not again until spring. If you're growing **fuchsias,** fertilizing them lightly will keep them blooming longer. Also keep watering them. Hybrid **roses,** which should be in their final full bloom, should be fed and their deep-watering continued; keep removing faded flowers and picking blooms to prevent seed set and prolong blooming. **Azaleas, camellias,** and **rhododendrons** are setting their buds; keep watering them. However, **camellias** should *not* be fertilized until spring. Also, discontinue fertilizing **tuberous begonias** to help the tubers resist rot while they're dormant, and allow the stems and leaves to die back.

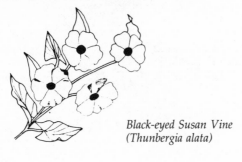

*Black-eyed Susan Vine
(Thunbergia alata)*

PREPARING FOR THE WINTER RAINS

If you have a tree with dense but brittle growth (i.e., Monterey pine) or a tree that puts out much thin whiplike growth (like evergreen Chinese elms), now is a good time to prune them back in preparation for the wind and storms of winter. Now is also the time to check roof gutters to make sure they're unblocked, as well as other water runoff systems. If one part of the garden stayed especially soggy last winter, you may want to create drainage paths.

By mid-October, **houseplants** should be moved back indoors for the winter (except jade plant, which can be out all year). Just remember to keep them in enough light.

HARVESTING

October is another prime harvesting month. **Tomatoes, eggplant, corn, zucchini,** and all the other warm-season vegetables you planted in early spring should be abundant now. (If you leave your green peppers on the plant a bit longer, they'll become sweet **red peppers.**) **Pumpkins** and **winter squash** should not be watered after their leaves turn yellow. **Walnuts** ripen in mid-October until the end of December. **Winter pears (Anjou, Bosc, Winter Nellis, Comice)** and **chestnuts** are available in the stores and are at their best now, early in the season. Mexican **Jim avocados** are available now through January; Mexican **Zutano avocados** are ripe now through December or even February. **Quinces** ripen late September through October, and **chayote** are ripe October through February. **Pineapple guavas** are harvestable now through November. **Saffron crocus** should be in flower, for harvesting saffron, and **rose hips** should also be collectable.

OCTOBER EVENTS

Oakland-East Bay Gardener Center Show—Lakeside Park, Oakland

Northern California Chapter National Chrysanthemum Society—Oakland Central Valley National Bank

Chrysanthemum Day—Lakeside Park, Oakland

Herb Day—Lakeside Park, Oakland

California Native Plant Society Sale—Merritt College, Oakland

Yamato Bonsai Club—Hayward

East Bay Bonsai Society—Lakeside Park, Oakland

Harvest Festival—Oakland Convention Center, Oakland

Harvest Fair—Martin Luther King Jr. Park, Berkeley

Harvest Festival—Brooks Hall, McAllister and Hyde Streets, San Francisco

Sunny Hills Grape Festival—Northgate Mall, Terra Linda exit off Hwy. 101, San Rafael

Pumpkin Festival—Half Moon Bay

Pumpkin Festival—Manteca

Harvest Fair—Sonoma County Fairgrounds, Santa Rosa

Oktoberfest—St. Joseph's Church, Pinole

Brussels Sprouts Festival—Santa Cruz

And, further afield, in the Central Valley:

Oktoberfest—Sacramento

Western Oktoberfest—Clovis (just north of Fresno)

Johnny Appleseed Days—Paradise (east of Chico)

Oktoberfest—Nevada County Fairgrounds, Grass Valley

Oktoberfest—Murphys (between Stockton and Yosemite)

Mountain Applefest—Golden Oak Mall, Road 426, Oakhurst (south of Yosemite)

Apple Hill Harvest Days (tour of 45 orchards and ranches)—east of Placerville (call El Dorado County Chamber of Commerce for information)

Pineapple Guava
(Feijoa sellowiana)

RECIPES

Chestnut Cheese Casserole

Serves 6

Chestnut trees, once a common street tree and important crop plant throughout the United States and Europe, have nearly disappeared from our gardens due to a disease epidemic. New resistant cultivars are being bred and may be available for planting soon, so that the next generation can once again enjoy this tasty nut. They are a Mediterranean plant, which would grow excellently in the East Bay. But for now, treat yourself to a taste experience by buying them at the store in *early* fall (not right before Thanksgiving) when they are fresh. This yummy dish is well worth the effort of shelling the chestnuts! (If it's a rainy fall and you're a mushroom hunter, you may get the rare joy of cooking this dish with early mushrooms as well.)

36 chestnuts (locally grown preferred, since they're usually fresher than imported; buy about 1 lb since you'll be throwing away a few bad ones)

2 large onions, thinly sliced

sharp cheddar cheese, shredded

1 small can evaporated milk

Sauce:

4 Tb butter

1 cup sliced mushrooms

2 green onions, finely chopped

2 cups sour cream

Garnish:

fresh or dried parsley

paprika

Slit each nutshell, and roast chestnuts about 45 minutes in a toaster oven or regular oven 15 to 20 minutes at 425 degrees. When cool enough, remove shell and as much of inner skin as possible (really difficult ones can be steamed slightly to help remove inner skin). Cut chestnuts as small as possible and place in a well-buttered glass casserole.

Top with sliced onions. Add a layer of cheese. Pour milk over all.

Bake at 375 degrees for 45 minutes.

Sauté mushrooms and green onions in butter until soft. Blend in sour cream, and spoon over casserole.

Garnish with minced parsley and paprika.

Hungarian Spiced Red Cabbage with Pears and Italian Arancini

Serves 4

A showcase dish for early fall pears, which are ripe and available now; if you live in a cool enough micro-climate, you may also have some summer-raised red cabbage to use. Cooking the Arancini is a chance to use some of the exotic saffron you may be harvesting from your saffron crocus plants. It's said to be much more tasty when fresh.

Spiced Red Cabbage with Pears

3 oz Canadian bacon
1 large onion, chopped
1 head red cabbage
2 or more cloves garlic, pressed or minced
1 Tb caraway seeds (optional)
1 tsp salt
¼ tsp pepper
2 large ripe pears, peeled if desired, chopped
1 lemon, halved
1–1½ cups red wine
3 Tb wine vinegar
3 Tb or less honey

Mince bacon and brown in a large pot. Add onion and simmer, stirring often, until softened.

Add cabbage, garlic, caraway, ½ cup warm water. Cover and cook until cabbage starts to soften.

Add salt, pepper, pears, lemon, wine, and vinegar. Cook uncovered 15 minutes.

Add honey. Cook over very low heat, covered, for 30 minutes. Check to see if cabbage is swimming in too much water. If so, uncover and cook until mostly steamed off.

Tastes even better if prepared a day ahead. A great leftover.

Arancini (Orange Cheese Rice Dumplings)

1 quart chicken stock (or 2 cans broth + 2 cans water)
2 cups Arborio ("risotto") rice (found in Italian markets) or other very sticky rice
¼ tsp saffron threads
½ cup freshly grated Parmesan cheese
3 Tb butter, *at room temperature*
salt and pepper to taste
2 eggs, beaten
6 oz mozzarella cheese, cut into 1-inch cubes
1 egg (or more), beaten
1½ cup dry bread crumbs
3 cups vegetable oil

Bring to a boil in a 4-quart pot the stock, rice, and saffron. Reduce heat and simmer 20 minutes or until all liquid is absorbed.

Stir in Parmesan, butter, salt, and pepper. Cool to room temperature. Blend in eggs.

With wet hands, roll each ½ cup of mixture into a 3-inch ball (about 13 of them); make indentations in each ball with thumb and insert a cube of mozzarella. Reroll ball to cover mozzarella.

Roll each ball in beaten egg, then in bread crumbs. (If desired, recipe can be stopped at this point, and balls stored in refrigerator until just before meal time.)

Heat oil in saucepan and deep-fry in batches until deep golden. Best served immediately.

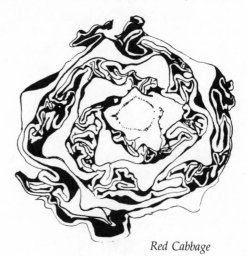

Red Cabbage

NOVEMBER

In November, the weather usually becomes unpredictable again. Though we may be unhappy with our umbrellas and boots, our plants love the rain. **Narcissus** and **mint** blooms may appear, and other plants perk up noticeably. The abrupt ending of Daylight Savings Time at the end of October makes the short days seem to come on disconcertingly fast. Even though November 7 is when winter officially commences, this month is actually our barely noticeable autumn in the East Bay, and by midmonth leaves are really changing color. The main show comes from bright red and orange liquidambars and Japanese and other maples; before they were planted for just this reason, the East Bay streets did not have much fall color at all. After Thanksgiving, the show will already be over, as the last leaves start to drop. Many plants also get purplish tinges to their leaves, as the colder nights do not allow all the starch produced during the day to get stored in their roots. (This usually makes vegetables taste sweeter.)

PLANTING

During stretches of drier weather you can keep interplanting cool-season vegetables; even if the rain and cold have started, it's still a good time to plant trees, perennials, and shrubs, giving them the benefit of a rainy season to get established. Winter- and spring-blooming annuals and a few bulbs (including **tulips** and **hyacinths**) can also still be planted. Biennials like **foxglove, Canterbury bell, sweet William, and Chinese forget-me-not** (*Cynoglossum*) can be included. Bare-root **asparagus** is best planted between now and March.

November is the prime time to shop for plants for fall color since you can actually view them in color now. At the end of November, nurseries should start to have **balled-and-burlapped** trees and shrubs:

Azaleas, rhododendrons, pines, spruces, and **conifers** are available for prices lower than they will be the rest of the year.

November is also the time to start **parsley** seeds for spring planting, since they take six weeks to germinate. Set them out between December and May.

FERTILIZING

Refrain from fertilizing almost everything now. Plants from colder climates need a dormant period in winter. The only exception might be the spring- and summer-flowering annuals or other newly bedded plants and cool-season vegetables you may have planted in September and October, and even they should be fertilized only lightly. Unless the rains are late, you can roll up your watering hose; you probably won't need it until next summer.

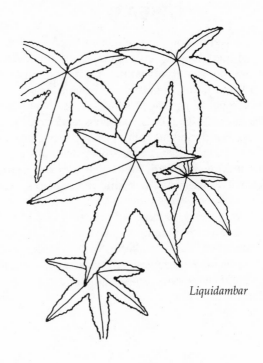

Liquidambar

Jade Plant
(Crassula argentea)

PRUNING

When the cool weather starts, you can prune **deciduous fruit trees** again, and it's a good time for renewing older fruit trees; however, you have until January to get any pruning done. The same is true of moving shrubs and trees, although you may want to root-prune in anticipation of moving them. Actually, it's better to put your energy into cleanup and removal right now. Spent **summer-flowering annuals** can be removed. (This is the traditional time to dig up **dahlias, gladiolus,** and **tuberous begonias** for over-winter storage, but in the East Bay we really don't need to do this.) Cut back and divide leggy perennials: **sages, geraniums, marguerites, fuchsias,** etc. Collect fallen leaves, and add them to your compost.

DISEASES

In the wet season, downy mildew becomes active (as opposed to powdery mildew). It's the yellow blotches on **sweet alyssum,** the grayish cast on **snapdragon,** and the purple cast on **onions.**

November is the time to spray for peach leaf curl, mites, scale, insect (i.e., aphid) eggs, and mealybugs on dormant deciduous fruit trees and roses, as well as berry bushes. Plants which may need this treatment include **almond, apple, apricot, cherry, nectarine,** and **peach, plum,** and **prune,** and other deciduous shade trees and shrubs. Copper sulfate ("Volck oil"), Bordeaux (copper) mix, or lime sulfur and oil are commonly used for this. Copper has now been found to affect protein synthesis and the production of enzymes in plants and cause stunting, so don't use this treatment without careful consideration of its necessity. Also, be sure not to hit any evergreens!

Fuchsia mite is what's likely to be hampering your **fuchsias.** There is little you can do about this recently arrived epidemic except spray. Redthread fungus becomes active on **Bermuda grass** just before it starts to go dormant, and botrytus fungus can cause red spots on the older flowers of **pink cyclamen.** Winter stress will begin to make visible the damage done by cypress tip moths on conifers such as **junipers, cypress,** and **arborvitae.** It appears as twig or branch dieback or as girdled branches.

If your redwood tree starts losing its needles right now, it may not be sick; it may be the deciduous **dawn redwood,** the ancestor of other redwoods, rediscovered in China in 1944 and brought to the Bay Area in 1948. One characteristic for identifying it from other redwoods is the "armpit" hollows on the trunk. It's a beautiful tree, but not an evergreen like the others.

GATHERING

November is usually the best time for mushroom hunting in the East Bay. The best way to determine the start of the mushroom season is to note the date of our first drenching rain (some time in September or October) and then make a mark on your calendar three weeks later. From that mark until the first frost is the mushroom season in the East Bay; usually November is the height of it. The exception is an offbeat year like 1986, with its nearly dry November and December; a prolonged dry spell after the first rains means a poor mushrooming year. But don't let it sadden you too much; the fungi will merely store up the energy they would have used to fruit, ready to release it as larger amounts of fruiting bodies (mushrooms) in the next good rainy year.

Even in a poor mushrooming year, golden orange and sometimes white or black **chantarelles** (*Cantharellus*), that gourmet treat, can be found in mounds in the leaf mulch under our native live oaks, rewarding their discoverer with a sweet, fruity ("apricot-y") smell and taste. If you do discover a patch of them, check back later in the winter; successive crops can be produced (sometimes all the way through to March).

Edible and delicious **oyster mushrooms** (*Pleurotus ostreatus*) start to appear in shelflike overlapping clusters on live or dead wood that gets wet enough. Bay trees are one of their favorite hosts, but they have been found growing on tan oaks, live oaks, cottonwoods, alders, sycamores, Lombardy poplars, willows, and maples. Said to be delicious rolled in bread crumbs and egg batter and fried, they also can produce several crops in one season from the same tree.

Another shelflike mushroom to watch for this month and next, this time on Douglas firs, is the **sulphur shelf** (see description under *August Gathering,* p. 60).

Another wet-weather lover is the **straw mushroom** (*Volvariella* family), which appears in compost piles that contain lots of fertilizer and straw. It is edible and closely related to the straw mushroom much used in Oriental cooking.

And if you've got an ailing oak tree, sick with oak root fungus (probably because it's growing in a lawn), you might make the best of it and enjoy the mushroom it puts out, with its highly rated taste. Young ones, picked before their gills open, are best, especially boiled or blanched first. Called **honey mushroom,** its botanical name was once *Armillaria,* and the disease is still commonly referred to by that name, but it has actually recently been reclassified as *Armallariella mellea,* and that's where you'll find it in mushroom guides. It's very variable in size, color, surface, and texture and can appear any time, but it is most abundant in fall and winter.

Old fruit trees, especially plums, may host an odd-looking mushroom, the **bear's head hericium** (*H. erinaceus*), which is white, covered with spines, and said to be very tasty.

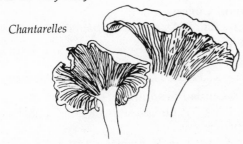

Chantarelles

HARVESTING

Persimmons are golden orange on bare branches from now into mid-December. You can bring them into the house to ripen; they're much better when the puckery bitterness turns to sweet cinnamon. (The Fuyu variety are edible and a tasty salad addition when still crisp.) Local **Granny Smith apples** are crisp and delicious. Cooking **pumpkins** ripen only in November, so now's the time for Pumpkin Pie or Pumpkin and White Bean Soup. **Bacon avocados** become available November to March; **Fuerte,** a

hybrid that is our most popular avocado, ripens November to June. **Kumquats** ripen November to June in Northern California. **Kiwis** grown in California are picked November to March.

Warm-climate fruit begin to appear in the market from southern areas. **Cherimoya** can be found from November to April. **Strawberry** and **lemon guava** (*Psidium guajava*) mature from November to February. **Pomegranates** and **mandarins** (including **Satsumas**) can be found now. **Navel oranges** are available especially in late November to May or June.

NOVEMBER EVENTS

RECIPES

Pumpkin and White Bean Soup

Serves 4

A hearty winter dinner.

½ lb Great Northern white beans

2 lb fresh pumpkin, skin removed, and cut into bite-size pieces (about one small pumpkin or the insides left over from carving out one medium-sized Jack o'Lantern*)

2 quarts chicken broth (2 14 oz cans + cans water)

2 carrots, sliced

4 leeks, sliced

1 sprig celery, sliced (optional)

3 Tb garlic, chopped

4 Tb marjoram

2 Tb thyme

1 to 1½ lemon, sliced

crusty French bread for dunking

Soak beans overnight.

Simmer beans and pumpkin in chicken broth for 1 hour.

Add other vegetables and herbs to soup, and cook 1 to 1½ hours more.

Add lemon slices last few minutes. Serve with bread.

* Rinse the pumpkin seeds for toasting (slowly in a moderately hot oven) and munching!

Persian Pomegranate Soup

Serves 4–6

The longer this soup sits, the better it gets. It's a delicious leftover.

1 onion, sliced
2 Tb butter
½ cup lentils
½ cup rice
½ cup parsley
½ lb spinach, washed and chopped
1 cup pomegranate juice or 2 large pomegranates
½ tsp oregano
1 tsp salt
¼ tsp pepper
Garnish:
fresh mint and coriander, chopped

Sauté onion in butter in heavy kettle until golden. Add lentils, cover with 8 cups of water, and bring to a boil; then lower heat, cover, and simmer for 30 minutes.

Meanwhile, extract juice from pomegranates by rolling them firmly but gently to mash seeds inside, then cutting a slit in their skin (fresher pomegranates work better for this).

Now add rice, parsley, spinach, pomegranate juice, oregano, salt, and pepper to the lentils. Simmer 45 minutes (at least); serve with garnish.

Pomegranates

PLANTS WHICH START TO BLOOM IN NOVEMBER AND DECEMBER

Trees

Loquat (*Eriobotrya japonica*): white
Red or Pink Ironbark (*Eucalyptus sideroxylon*): pink
Sweet Hakea (*Hakea suaveolens*): white bottlebrush
New Zealand Tea Tree/Manuka (*Leptospermum scoparium*): white or pink or rosy red
 (cv. 'Ruby Glow' is brilliant red)
 (blooms through much of the year, but is especially noticeable in winter)

Shrubs

Azalea (some cvs.) (*Rhododendron* sp.): many colors
Camellia japonica (some cvs.): white, pinks, reds
Camellia sasanqua (some cvs.): white, pinks, reds
Black-Eyed Heather (*Erica canaliculata*): showy dark pink or rose-purple teeny bells
Golden Shrub Daisy (*Euryops pectinatus*): yellow daisylike
Pincushion Tree (*Hakea laurina*): red bottlebrush
Chinese Hibiscus (*Hibiscus rosa-sinensis*): many colors
Burmese Mahonia (*Mahonia lomarifolia*): yellow, at the same time as blue-violet and lavender fruit
Laurustinus (*Viburnum tinus*): pink buds and white flowers, at the same time as blue-black fruit

Ground Covers

Trailing African Daisy (*Osteospermum fruticosm*): purple + white

Vines

Primrose Jasmine (*Jasminum mesnyi*): yellow

Herbaceous Perennials

Natal Lily (*Clivia miniata*): orange-red funnel with yellow throat
Jade Plant (*Crassula argentea*): tiny white
Corsican Hellebore (*H. lividus-corsicus*): chartreuse
Christmas Rose (*Hellebore niger*): white-purplish
Bird-of-Paradise (*Strelitzia reginae*): blue + orange + white (blooms throughout year, but best in cold weather)

Annuals

Pot Marigold (*Calendula officinalis*): orange, yellow + cvs.
English Primrose (*Primula x polyantha*): many colors
Viola (*V. cornuta*): violet (+ cvs.)
Johnny-Jump-Up (*Viola tricolor*): violet + gold + white

Pansy (*Viola x wittrockiana*): many colors, usually with contrasting markings at the petal base

Bulbs
"Florists" Cyclamen (*C. persicum*): crimson, red, salmon, purple, white
Daffodils and Jonquils (*Narcissus* sp.): white
Nerine bowdenii: pink

"DEPENDABLE" FALL FOLIAGE COLOR
(These plants can be counted on to have nice fall color even in the East Bay's mild climate.)

Trees
Maples (*Acer* sp.): oranges, reds, yellows
Catalpa sp.: yellows
Dogwoods (*Cornus* species, including the native Redtwig Dogwood, *C. stolonifera,* the bare stems of which turn brilliant red)
Persimmons (*Diospyros kaki*): yellows, oranges, or scarlets
Honey Locust (*Gleditsia triacanthos*): yellow
Maidenhair Tree (*Ginkgo biloba*): yellow
Goldenrain Tree (*Koelreuteria paniculata*): yellow to orange to red (less showy than in colder climates)
Crape Myrtle (*Lagerstroemia indica*): yellow to orange to red (less showy than in colder climates)
Sweet Gum (*Liquidambar styraciflua*): orange, yellow
Tulip Tree (*Liriodendron tulipifera*): bright yellow

Chinese Pistache (*Pistacia chinensis*): scarlet, crimson, orange, or yellow (+ red fruit on female plants)
Lombardy Poplar (*Populus nigra* 'Italica'): brown with yellow
Flowering Plum (*Prunus blireiana*): red (burgundy to purple)
Japanese Flowering Cherry (*Prunus serrulata*): showy yellow to orange
Flowering Pear (*Pyrus kawakamii*): yellow + red (very briefly)
Chinese Tallow Tree (*Sapium sebiferum*): brilliant red!
American Elm (*Ulmus americana*): brown to yellow
Sawleaf Zelkova (*Zelkova serrata*): gorgeous red + yellow

Shrubs
Heavenly Bamboo (*Nandina domestica*): reds
Chinese Photinia (*Photinia serrulata*): crimson
Pomegranate (*Punica granatum*): bright yellow
Staghorn Sumac (*Rhus typhina*): bright red

Vines
Kiwi (*Actinidia chinensis*): yellow
Boston Ivy (*Parthenocissus tricuspidata*): showy orange to red
Also Virginia Creeper (*P. quinquefolia*)

Strawberries

DECEMBER

December brings wintry winds, and the cold intensifies. Trees are becoming bare, and fallen leaves drift onto cars and the street. It's no surprise that traditionally this is a time for indoor feasts, parties, and gatherings. Some **azaleas** and **camellias** should be brightening the garden by now; water-loving **heathers** (*Erica*) are in their glory (feathery bushes covered with dark pink tiny blossoms). **Heavenly bamboo** (*Nandina*) is at its peak of brilliant red color now, reacting to the sun and the cold. The other bright splash outdoors is **New Zealand tea tree,** especially the neon rose red Ruby Glow cultivar much planted around the East Bay. A very common plant in East Bay gardens also in full bloom now (from November to March) is the **jade plant,** though its small but profuse white blooms are more noticeable close up.

December and January are the most likely months for frost. This little rhyme tells how to predict it: "The windshield's dry, the stars are in sight; the trees are all quiet, expect frost tonight." But in the East Bay, our winter is so short that it collapses into spring. The turning point of the year, Midwinter's Day, the Winter Solstice (shortest day and longest night), is December 22. Spring is just around the corner. Put out a bird feeder, and help those birds get through the coldest months of the year.

PLANTING

This is *not* a good time for planting; digging wet soil is not a wise practice, even if you wanted to work in the cold and rainy weather. But it is *the* prime month to buy **bare-root trees** and **shrubs**. Fruit and nut trees such as **almond, apple, apricot, fig, nectarine, pear, peach, persimmon, plum, pomegranate, quince,** and **walnut** are cheaper and freshly available now. Also available bare-root are **roses, flowering quince, rose-of-Sharon,** *Weigela,* **wisteria,** and many ornamental trees; plus food crops such as **artichokes, asparagus, caneberries, (boysen, logan, olallie), kiwi, rhubarb, strawberries,** and **grapes.** You can also select **azaleas** and **camellias** now, while they're in bloom. Bulbs bought now may well be the poorer quality leftovers, although they can still be planted, and this is a likely time for sales. Get out your seed catalogs, sit by the fire, and plan next year's garden!

PRUNING AND MAINTENANCE

The end-of-the-month holidays are an excellent time to **prune deciduous plants**; see *January Pruning,* p. 28, for more information. Cold crisp weather keeps the pathogen activity low; most deciduous trees are fully bare. This is the time the city gardeners "pollard" the London plane trees on streets and public grounds to keep them small. You may see them on your street.

December 15 is the last chance for dormant-spraying of deciduous plants that have pest or disease problems (*see November Diseases,* p. 74).

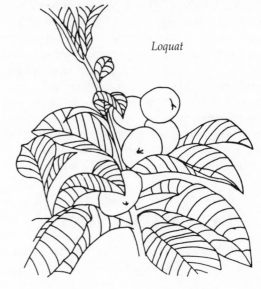

Loquat

Cauliflower, cabbage, and **broccoli** planted last fall begin to form heads now; commercial farmers tie the leaves up around their cauliflower heads now to keep them white, but actually they are more nutritious and flavorful if allowed to turn green.

Fruit tree growers should be thankful for cold weather now; warm weather in December can make apples leaf out, possibly resulting in later fruit loss.

GATHERING

If you're keeping a compost pile going now, you may find edible **blewits** (*Lepista nuda*), pretty purplish-blue mushrooms, in it now or into January. They are deep violet fading to pinkish-tan and often grow in fairy rings or arcs. They can be found in brambles under live oaks or almost anywhere there is a good amount of organic debris. They are best cooked with milk and cream.

Young pine trees may host another edible mushroom, **black elfin saddle** (*Helvella lacunosa*), during these cold months; it is black with no gills and a white stem full of holes. It is said to be tasty when cooked, although somewhat chewy; drying and lightly crushing it are said to make it better for culinary use.

HARVESTING

Now is the prime time for **citrus** to fruit (orange, grapefruits, tangerines). There are only a few varieties that fruit well in the Bay Area (check with Four Winds Nursery in Fremont for suggestions: 656–2591), but a December trip to Palm Springs, Indio, and the Coachella Valley should put you in the heart of its growing area. **Kumquats** ripen from November to June in Northern California; they should also be plentiful in the stores now. If your garden was started in September and October, many leafy **cool-season vegetables** should be starting to be harvestable now. If you only harvest individual green tops from your **green onions,** they will continue to put on new green shoots, and you'll have them fresh for much longer. **Broccoli, cabbage,** and **artichokes** will develop additional heads if you cut the mature ones off.

DECEMBER EVENTS

San Francisco Garden Club Winter Flower Show—Golden Gate Park Hall of Flowers

Hibiscus

RECIPES

Pot au Feu (French Fire Pot)

Serves 4

The special taste of this traditional French winter soup/stew comes from the combination of turnips and marjoram. Turnips from a fall-planted garden should be harvestable soon, and your marjoram has probably perked up with the winter rains.

1 each hot, sweet, and Polish sausages
1 onion, cut into bite-size pieces
3 whole cloves
2 or more cloves garlic, minced or pressed
2–3 bay leaves
1 tsp thyme
½ tsp pepper
salt to taste
parsley sprigs
celery leaf sprigs
dash of allspice
½–1 tsp marjoram, fresh or dried
½ cup wine

2 turnips or rutabagas
2 potatoes
2 carrots
3 leeks
optional: ½ head cabbage, 1–2 stalks celery, ¼–½ lb mushrooms, 1–2 Tb lemon juice

Sauté onions and garlic; add all seasonings and the wine and cook in a large pot for 1 to 2 hours.

Cut up and add the vegetables (the smaller they're cut, the faster they'll cook) for the last 30 minutes.

Belgian Horseradish Sauce for Pot au Feu:
3 Tb prepared horseradish, undrained
1 Tb prepared mustard
3 Tb lemon juice
½ tsp salt
1 cup sour cream

Combine all ingredients and serve with Pot Au Feu.

Persimmon Cookies or Bread

Makes about 60 cookies or 2 loaves

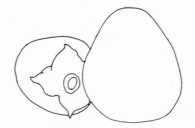

Hachiya Persimmon

½ cup sugar
½ cup butter, *at room temperature*
⅓ cup milk (or ⅙ cup if making bread)
1 egg
1 cup very ripe persimmons, skinned
1 cup chopped nuts (peanuts are great)
1 cup raisins (optional)
2 cups flour (up to 1 cup can be whole wheat)
1 tsp baking powder
¼ tsp salt
½ tsp cloves
½ tsp cinnamon

Cream together butter and sugar. Beat in milk, egg, persimmon, nuts, and raisins.

Sift together flour, baking powder, and spices. Fold dry ingredients into wet mixture, and blend.

Drop on greased cookie sheet and bake at 350 degrees for 10 –15 minutes. Or pour into 2 greased loaf pans, and bake at 350 degrees 1 to 1½ hours, until slightly browned on outside.

EAST BAY GARDENERS' RESOURCE GUIDE

SOILS, AMENDMENTS, COMPOST, AND MULCHES
(listed from north to south)

Hasenflug's Topsoil & Rock Co.
3232 San Pablo Dam Road, San Pablo
232-4799 or 223-5195

Am Soil
2222 Third St. (at Bancroft), Berkeley
540-8011

U-Save
9317 MacArthur Blvd., Oakland
578-3072

Clarks Home and Garden Building Materials
23040 Clawiter Road, Hayward
783-6366

Free Mulch:
Davey Tree, Livermore
(800) 972-5261

Free Leaf Mold:
Piedmont Corporation Yard
898 Moraga Avenue, Piedmont
420-3065

Rice Hulls:
Greenwood Gardens
636 San Pablo Ave., Pinole
724-5091

Cocoa Bean Hulls:
Guittard Chocolate, Burlingame
697-4427
(only $1 per bag, although you must take 50 bags)

Spent Hops (from beer production):
Roaring Rock Brewery
1920 Shattuck, Berkeley
843-2739

Spent Hops and Grains:
Thousand Oaks Brewing Co., Berkeley
525-8801

Manure:
Nitabell Rabbitry
29215 Taylor Avenue, Hayward
782-4655

Many local stables have Horse Manure, free if you load it yourself, including:
East Bay Regional Park District Equestrian Center
569-4428
Tilden Park Pony Ride
527-0421
Piedmont Stables
531-9944
Vista Madera Stables
562-4087

Cow Manure:
Horner Meat Co.
2500 Davis Street, San Leandro
568-7274

Zoo Doo:
Available from the San Francisco Zoo in bulk,
at many Bay Area nurseries, or at
Urban Resources Systems, Inc.
783 Buena Vista Ave. West
San Francisco, CA 94117
621-3260

Sawdust (use only hardwood dust, no particleboard or plywood; redwood dust will acidify the soil):
Many local lumberyards, including:
Truitt & White Lumber
Second and Hearst, Berkeley
841-0511 (free)

El Cerrito Mill, 10812 San Pablo Avenue, El Cerrito
525-0220 (sold by the bag or truckload)

EARTHWORMS
The Earthworm Company
3675 Calistoga Road, Santa Rosa 95404
(707) 539-6335

Nitabell Rabbitry
29215 Taylor Avenue, Hayward
782-4655

ORGANIC GARDENING SUPPLIES
The Ecology Center
1403 Addison Street, Berkeley (behind Co-op store)
548-2220

Connecticut Street Plant Supplies
306 Connecticut Street, San Francisco
(on Potrero Hill)
821-4773

Common Ground
2225 El Camino Real, Palo Alto
328-6752

FRUIT CULTIVARS FOR THE EAST BAY CLIMATE
Peaceful Valley Farm Supply
11173 Peaceful Valley Road, Nevada City,
CA 95959
(916) 265-3339
(Sells stock produced by Dave Wilson Nursery,
which no longer sells retail, including
Floyd Zaiger dwarfs)

Fowler Nurseries
525 Fowler Road, Newcastle, CA 95658

Harmony Farm Supply
P.O. Box 451, Graton, CA 95444
(707) 823-9125

Living Tree Centre
P.O. Box 797, Bolinas, CA 94924
868-1786
(heritage fruit trees)

Sonoma Antique Apple Nursery
4395 Westside Road, Healdsburg, CA 95448
(707) 433-6420
(antique fruit trees)

Emil Lindquist, San Pablo
233-1245
(pome fruit trees, berries)

Dwarf Citrus:
Four Winds Nursery
42186 Palm Ave., Fremont
656-2591

Native Plants:
DAWN (Design Advocates Working with Nature)
Spinnaker Way, Berkeley
644-1315

Las Pilitas Nursery
Star Route, P.O. Box 23, Santa Margarita, CA 93453

NURSERIES WITH GOOD SELECTIONS
(listed from north to south)

Adachi Nursery
11939 San Pablo Ave., El Cerrito
235-6352

Anthony J. Skittone
2271 31st Ave., San Francisco, CA 94116
(unusual bulbs and plants; write for catalog)

Berkeley Hort Nursery
1310 McGee, Berkeley
526-4704

East Bay Nursery
2332 San Pablo, Berkeley
845-6490

Magic Gardens Nursery
729 Heinz Ave., Berkeley
644-1992, 644-2351

Dwight Way Nursery
1001 Dwight Way, Berkeley
845-6261

Evergreen Nursery
1057 MacArthur, San Leandro
632-1522

Ole's Home Center
300 Floresta Blvd., San Leandro
483-4811

Orchard Supply Hardware
177 Lewelling Blvd., San Leandro
278-1336

West Nursery
13760 East 14th Street, San Leandro

Fuji's Plant Outlet
24949 Soto Road at Orchard, Hayward
886-1577

Mission Adobe Nursery (formerly California
Nursery Co.)
36501 Niles, Fremont
796-7575

Sunol Nursery
Hwy. 680 & Calaveras Road, Fremont

And, a little further afield (Contra Costa County):
Orchard Nursery & Florist
4010 Mount Diablo Blvd., Lafayette
284-4474

Windy Hill Nursery
Old Tunnel Road & Buchan Drive, Lafayette
934-3406

Navlet's
1250 Monument Blvd., Concord
685-0700

SOME SOURCES FOR SEEDS FOR THE EAST BAY

(Seeds purchased from seed-sources nearby or in similar climate zones are best adapted.)

Nearby:
Heirloom Garden Seeds
P.O. Box 138, Guerneville, CA 95446

Fowler Nurseries
525 Fowler Road, Newcastle, CA 95658

J.L. Hudson, Seedsman
P.O. Box 1058, Redwood City, CA 94064

Le Marche Seeds International
P.O. Box 566, Dixon, CA 95620

Redwood City Seed Company
P.O. Box 361, Redwood City, CA 94604

Shepherd's Garden Seeds
7389 West Zayante Road, Felton, CA 95018

In Similar Climate Zones:
Abundant Life Seed Foundation
P.O. Box 772, Port Townsend, WA 98368

Casa Yerba Gardens
Star Route 2, Box 21, Days Creek, OR 97429

ForestFarm
990 Tetherow Road, Williams, OR 97544

Nichols Garden Nursery
1190 North Pacific Hwy., Albany, OR 97321

Territorial Seed Company
P.O. Box 27, Lorane, OR 97451

Forgot to order ahead?
Navlet's Oakland store
520 20th Street
has a good selection of the cultivars recommended for the East Bay.

Sources for California Natives:
Larner Seeds
P.O. Box 60143, Palo Alto, CA 94306

Theodore Payne Foundation
10459 Tuxford Street, Sun Valley, CA 91352

NEIGHBORHOOD TREE PLANTINGS

On Top
Oakland
c/o 273-3151

Friends of the Urban Forest
512 Second Street, San Francisco
543-5000

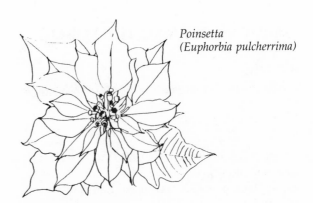

Poinsetta
(Euphorbia pulcherrima)

INFORMATION

Ecology Center
1403 Addison Street (behind Co-op store), Berkeley
548-2220

Merritt College Horticulture Department
12500 Campus Drive, Oakland
436-2418

San Francisco League of Urban Gardeners (SLUG)
515 Cortland Avenue, San Francisco
695-9100

U.C. Agriculture Co-op Extension
224 W. Winton Avenue, Hayward, CA 94544
881-6341
or Campus Public Service Offices
2120 University Avenue, Berkeley, CA 94720
644-4345

U.C. Forestry Department
2120 University Avenue, Berkeley

Integrated Pest Management
The Bio Integral Resource Center
P.O. Box 7414, Berkeley, CA 94707
524-2567

California Native Plant Society
909 12th Street, Suite 116
Sacramento, CA 95814

San Francisco Mycological Society
P.O. Box 11321, San Francisco 94101
759-0495

California Rare Fruit Growers
c/o Fullerton Arboretum
California State University
Fullerton, CA 92634

Indoor Citrus and Rare Fruit Society
176 Coronado Ave., Los Altos, CA 94022

Garden Clubs:
Call Lakeside Park Garden Center
832-9329 for information on meeting times and events

GARDENS OPEN TO THE PUBLIC

(from north to south)

Blake Estate
Rincon Road, Kensington (between Berkeley and El Cerrito)
(open weekdays only)

Strybing Arboretum
Golden Gate Park, San Francisco

Berkeley Municipal Rose Garden
Euclid Avenue at Bayview Place, Berkeley

East Bay Regional Parks Botanical Garden
(California native plants)
Tilden Regional Park

University of California Botanical Garden
Centennial Drive, Berkeley

Mountain View Cemetery
5000 Piedmont Avenue, Oakland

Kaiser Secret Rooftop Garden
Webster and 21st Street, Oakland
(This private garden including a reflecting pool and swans is for Kaiser employees, but the public is not barred. Go south on Webster and turn left onto Grand Avenue; turn right immediately onto Kaiser Plaza and park. Walk to end of Kaiser Plaza and continue around building to the left until you find a parking structure stairway which is open. Walk up to roof. Don't tell too many friends about this one.)

Oakland Rose Garden (Morcom Amphitheatre of Roses)
Jean and Olive Streets, Oakland

Lakeside Park Gardens
west edge of Lake Merritt, Oakland

Dunsmuir House
Peralta Oaks Court, Oakland

Villa Montalvo Arboretum
Montalvo Road, Saratoga

Hakone Japanese Garden
Big Basin Way, Saratoga

CULTIVARS FOR THE EAST BAY CLIMATE

Starred cultivars (*) have gotten especially high ratings by East Bay gardeners.

VEGETABLES

Beans: Pole: *'Kentucky Wonder'
  *'Romano'
  'Blue Lake'
  *'Scarlet Runner'
  'Provider'
  Bush: most, i.e. 'Contender'
  'Burpee's Greensleeves'
  'Rust-resistant Golden Wax'
  'Royalty Burpee'
  (Bush beans give less return than pole beans, but don't have to be staked and ripen sooner.)
  *Fava/Broad: any

Beets: 'Detroit Dark Red'
  'Early Wonder'
  'Ruby Queen'
  'Golden Beet'

*Broccoli: 'Italian Green Sprouting'
  'Green Comet'

Brussels Sprouts: 'Jade Cross'

Cabbage: 'Early Jersey Wakefield' (green; for fall planting)
  'Earliana' (for fall planting)
  'Savoy King' (for spring planting)
  'Ball Head' (for spring planting)
  'Mammoth Red Rock' (red)
  Chinese Cabbage/Bok Choy

Carrots: Shorter-length carrots do better in our clay soils.
  *'Chantenay'
  'Danvers Half Long'
  'Half Longs'
  'Oxheart'

Cauliflower: 'Burpeeana'
  'Purple Head'
  'Self Blanche'
  'Snowball'

Celery: most, i.e., 'Self-blanching'

Chard: all, i.e., 'Rhubarb', 'Fordhook Giant', 'French Swiss'

Collards: all, i.e., 'Georgia', 'Vates'

Corn: most
    Be sure to plant a block of at least four rows for pollination!
    Try planting cultivars that ripen at different times for harvest throughout the summer.
    Some successes:
    Early ripeners—
    *'Early Sunglow'
    'Golden Beauty'
    Middle ripeners—
    'Burpee Golden Bantam'
    'Tendermost'
    'Burpee's Honeycross'
    'Jubilee'
    For a late-starting crop—''Silver Queen'
        *'Illini Extra Sweet'

Cucumbers: 'Saladin'
    'Sweet Slice'
    *'Lemon' ("more for the space")
    'Japanese Climbing'
    Pickling Cucumbers, i.e., 'Burpee Pickler'
    *'Burpee's Bush Spacemaster'

Eggplant: Japanese (i.e., 'Ichiban')
    'Dusky'
    'Black Beauty'
    'Black Magic'

Endive: all

Garlic: all

Kale: all, i.e., 'Curley Scotch'
    'Hanover'

Leeks: 'American Flag'

Lettuce: *'Oak Leaf'
    'Black Seeded Simpson'
    'Ruby Red'
    'Salad Bowl'
    'Royal Oak'
    'Kentucky Limestone' (for fall planting)
    'Butter' or 'Great Lakes' (for spring planting)
        'Romaine' or 'Red' (for fall planting; not spring!)
    'Butter Crunch' (very good)

Melons (grow in a cold frame):
    'Minnesota Midget' cantaloupe
    'Golden Midget' watermelon
    (A few areas can grow cantaloupes outdoors.)

Mustard: all

Onions (bulbing): most, i.e., 'Sweet Spanish'
    'Torpedo'
    'Red Spanish'

Onions (bunching): 'White Bunching'

Peas: *'Sugar Snap' (a cross between a snow pea and a regular pea; whole pod is edible)
    'Mammoth Melting Pod/Sugar Pea' (for fall planting)
    also 'Dwarf Grey Sugar'
earliest spring-planting: 'Burpeeana'
    'Blue Wonder'
mid- to late-spring-planting: 'Fordhook Wonder'

Peppers (Hot)/Chiles: most, i.e., Jalapeno, Anaheim, Thai

Peppers (Sweet): *'Yolo Wonder'

Potatoes: most, i.e. 'Red Lasado', 'White Rose'

Radishes: most, i.e., 'Crimson Giant,' 'French Breakfast'

Rhubarb: all

Spinach: 'Melody'
    'All America'
    'Bloomsdale Long Standing' (for spring planting)
    'Winter Bloomsdale' (for fall planting)

Squash (Summer): Zucchini, Crookneck

Squash (Winter): Acorn, Banana, Butternut, Hubbard (winter squash take a bit longer to mature)
    Pumpkin: most, i.e., 'Big Max', 'Triple Threat', 'Cinderella Bush'

Tomatoes: (VF and VFN indicate resistance to verticillium wilt)
    'Ace'
    'Arctic'
    'Beefsteak'
    *'Better Boy' (VFN)
    'Big Boy'
    'Big Early'
    'VF Burpee Hybrid'
    'Burpee's Basket Pack' (cherry)
    *'Coldset' (highly recommended)
    'Champion'
    *'Early Girl' (also wilt resistant)
    'Jubilee' (yellow)
    *'Patio' (smaller fruit)
    'Pearson Improved'
    'Pixie' (smaller fruit, early ripening)
    'Quick Pick'
    *'Red Cherry'

*'VF Roma' (can get wilt resistant strains, though fruit ripens early, so it may not matter; smaller fruit)

'Rutgers'

'San Marzano' (Italian pear-shaped, late ripener)

'Small Fry'

'Spring Giant'

'Stupice'

'Supersteak'

*'Sweet 100' (cherry)

'Tiny Tim' (cherry)

'Whopper'

'Yellow Pear'

('San Francisco Fog' sets fruit, but is said not to be very tasty.)

*Tomatillos: all

*Watercress: all (needs very moist spot, preferably a pool or running stream, so not suitable for most garden plots)

FRUITS AND NUTS

Apples: tart varieties do best
 'Golden Delicious' (harvest mid- to late-season)
 'Gordon' (recent cultivar from Southern California) (long fruiting season)
 'Granny Smith' (ripens November/late-season)
 'Gravenstein' (early-season)
 'Jonathan' (mid-season)
 'Newtown Pippin'/'Pippin' (late-season)
 'Sweet Delicious'

Emil Lindquist suggests:
Hudson's 'Golden Gem' (yellow russet, sweet)
'Gala' (red sweet)
'Red Fireside' (sweet)

Apricots: must be pollinated if there is a rainy spring; treat while in full bloom with 'Harmax' from Brooker Chemical, P.O. Box 9335 Hollywood, CA 91606 (suggested by Emil Lindquist)
 'Royal' ('Blenheim')
 'Moorpark'

Avocados: any

Berries: Blackberry (including Boysen, Logan, Olallie; Olallie is the heaviest bearer)
 (These are all less invasive than the 'Himalaya' cultivar developed by Luther Burbank which has taken over backyards.)
 Currants
 Elderberry
 Gooseberry
 Huckleberry
 Raspberry: especially nice are "two-crop varieties" i.e., 'Newberg'; 'September or Indian Summer'
 Serviceberry
 Strawberry: most, i.e., 'Sequoia', 'Tioga', 'Ever-bearing'
 An older strawberry cultivar, 'Shasta', did better than any of these, but is hard to find now; it is available from Fowler Nurseries, 525 Fowler Road, Newcastle CA 95658

Cherries: sour varieties do best
 'Montmorency'
 'Nanking Bush Cherry' (*Prunus tomentosa*) (fruit has almost no stem, so birds have trouble getting it; mostly used as a dwarf rootstock for plums)
 One sweet cherry that does okay is 'Bing'; however, it is sterile and needs a pollinator (Van or Tartarian), so you have to have room for 2 trees.

Figs: 'Italian Everbearing'

Grapes: 'Black Malukkah'
 'Concord'
 'Thompson Seedless'

Lemon: 'Eureka'
 'Meyer' ('Improved' is the only kind that can legally be sold since it is the only kind immune to the Quick Decline virus.)

Lime: 'Bearss' Lime'
 'Rangpur Lime'

Loquat: any

Nectarines: Emil Lindquist suggests 'Tiger'

Nuts: Almond
   Chestnut
   Macadamia
   Walnut (although it gets Walnut Blight)

Olive: any

Oranges: Mandarins, i.e., 'Owari Satsuma'
   Blood Orange (in warmer areas)
   Navel Orange (in warmer areas)
   Emil Lindquist suggests 'Valencia Trovita' (dwarf or standard) available from Four Winds Nursery in Fremont.

Peaches: Emil Lindquist suggests 'Redhaven' (yellow), 'Champion', and 'Southern Belle' (both white).

Pears: any, including Asian Pears

Persimmon: any (Fuyu said to be outstanding)

Plums: most, including Japanese

Pomegranate

Quince: any

Subtropicals: Strawberry Guava (*Psidium littoral*)
   Pineapple Guava (*Feijoa sellowiana*)
   Cherimoya (*Annona cherimoia*)
   Jujube/Chinese Date (*Zizyphus jujube*)
   Kiwi/Chinese Gooseberry (*Actinidia chinensis*) (needs both sexes for fruit)
   Loquat (*Eriobotrya japonica*)
   Natal Plum (*Carissa grandiflora*)
   Sapote (*Casimiroa edulis*)
   Surinam Cherry (*Eugenia uniflora*)

EDIBLE ORNAMENTALS

The following plants grow in the East Bay and have edible fruit (or other edible parts as noted), but are currently grown mainly as ornamentals (edible but not tasty plants are also noted, in case a future Luther Burbank is reading):

Shrubs:

Roses (especially *R. rugosa*; great for rose hips)
many Mahonia species
Pyracantha (not tasty)
Chilean Guava (*Ugni molinae*)
Silverberry (*Eleagnus pungens*)
Pink-Flowering Currant (*Ribes sanguineum glutinosm*)
Manzanita
Natal Plum
Fuchsia-Flowered Gooseberry (*Ribes speciosum*; peel annoying skin)
Snowberry (not tasty)

Trees:

Digger Pine
Carob (puts seed pods out in the spring, heaviest every second year)
Mulberry
Loquat
Australian Brush Cherry (*Syzigium paniculatum*, once called *Eugenia*; can be bush or tree)
Crabapple
Dogwood (not tasty)
Strawberry Tree (*Arbutus unedo*)
Fern Pine (*Podocarpus gracilior*)
Yew Pine (*P. macrophyllus*)
Chinquapin
Oak (after tannin is removed)
Bay (olivelike fruit can be roasted)
Coffeeberry (not tasty)
Lemonade Berry (*Rhus integrifolia*)
Sugarbush (*Rhus ovata*)
Islay or Holly-Leaf Cherry (*Prunus ilicifolia*)
Madrone
Western Hazelnut/Filbert
Blue Elderberry (can be shrub or tree)

Ground Covers:

Salal
Bearberry/Kinnikinnick
Yerba Buena (leaves used for delicious tea)
Sea Fig or Hottentot Fig (*Carpobrotus edulis*; the standard iceplant)

Vines:

Passion Vine (*Passiflora edulis*)
Fiveleaf Akebia/Chocolate Vine (*Akebia quinata*)

Herbaceous and Flowering Plants, Weeds:

Red Valerian (*Centranthus ruber*; leaves can be used in salad or as a cooked vegetable; roots are used in soups in France; flowers)
Sweet Alyssum (*Lobularia maritima*; greens)
English Daisy (greens, flowers)
Epazote (cook greens with beans)
Milk Thistle (*Silybum marianum*; peel and eat stalks; young shoots use for salad greens; roots eat like salsify; heads boil and eat like artichokes)
Yellow Nut Sedge/Umbrella Plant (tubers edible after roasting)
Weeds listed under *March Harvesting*, p. 37 (greens)

PLANTING TIMES FOR THE EAST BAY

To supplement the preferred planting times given in the text, this is a more precise guide to exactly which months plants can be set out. This chart shows the very earliest and latest dates to set out plants during the main planting seasons, in case you have to plant late or want to plant early. Unless otherwise noted, planting dates are for plants started from seed. In general, sow seeds 6–7 weeks earlier than you wish to set out seedlings.

"COOL-SEASON" CROPS:

Beans (Fava)	Nov + Feb–Apr
Broccoli	Feb–Mar + June–Sept (plants only after Aug 1)
Brussels Sprouts	Apr–July + Sept–Nov
Cabbage	Jan–Nov (plants only after Aug 1)
Chinese Cabbage	July–Aug
Cauliflower	Jan–May + Aug–Nov
Celery	Feb–May + Aug–Nov
Chard	all year
Endive	Mar–July + Sept–Nov
Garlic	Aug–Mar 15
Kale	Jan–Feb + Sept–Oct
Kohlrabi	Mar–Apr + Sept–Nov
Lettuce (leaf)	Jan–Nov
Lettuce (cos)	Mar–Apr
Mustard	July–Nov
Parsnips	Apr–July + Sept–Nov
Radish	all year
Rutabaga	Sept–Nov
Spinach	Feb–June + Aug–Nov 15
Turnips	Jan–June + Aug–Dec

"IN-BETWEEN" CROPS:

Chives	Feb–Apr
Parsley	Dec–May

"WARM-SEASON" CROPS:

Beans	May–July
Beets	Feb–Nov
Carrots	Jan–Nov
Celeriac	Mar–June
Corn (sweet)	Apr–July 15
Cucumber	May 1–July 15
Eggplant	May (plants)
Jer. Artichokes	Sept–Nov + Jan–Mar (nonseed)
Leek	Feb–Apr + June + Sept–Nov
Onions	Oct–Apr (sets)
Peas	Jan–Nov
Peppers	May (plants)
Potatoes (white)	Jan–Aug (nonseed) + Sept–Nov
Pumpkins	May–June
Squash	May–July (summer squash) May–June (winter squash)
Sunflower	Apr–July 15
Tomatoes	Apr–May (plants)

PERENNIAL CROPS:

Artichoke	Aug–Dec (nonseed)
Asparagus	Jan–Feb (roots)
Chayote	Jan–Mar (nonseed)
Rhubarb	Sept–March

INDEX

PLANT INDEX

SUBJECT INDEX

RECIPE INDEX

Photograph: Peggy Stokes